Praise for
The New Book of Wedding Etiquette . . .

❧

"An outstanding resource for anyone planning a wedding! Shaw's advice is concise, on target, in good taste, and always full of dry humor!"

CAROLYN SHEPARD-BAEHRE, AIFD, PRESIDENT,
CAROLYN SHEPARD DESIGN GROUP

❧

"As a wedding planner, Shaw is known for her elegant style and creative flair—and these attributes shine throughout the book."

LIZ NEELY, PUBLISHER, *CAROLINA BRIDE* MAGAZINE

❧

"Easy to navigate and a must-read for all newly engaged couples."

JILL MARCUS, MANAGING PARTNER,
SOMETHING CLASSIC CATERING & GOURMET SHOPPES

KIM SHAW

THE NEW BOOK OF
WEDDING
ETIQUETTE

How to Combine the Best Traditions
with Today's Flair

THREE RIVERS PRESS • NEW YORK

Certain suggestions are made in this book. While these are intended to be helpful to the reader, the reader must assume all risk associated with following any particular suggestion. Therefore, in purchasing this book, the reader agrees that the author and publisher are not liable or responsible for any injury or damage caused by the use of any information contained herein.

All of the characters in this book are based on real persons. Any resemblance to actual persons, living or dead, is purely coincidental, unless authorized by the actual person mentioned.

Published by Three Rivers Press, New York, New York.
Member of the Crown Publishing Group, a division of Random House, Inc.
www.crownpublishing.com

THREE RIVERS PRESS and the Tugboat design are registered trademarks of Random House, Inc.

Originally published by Prima Publishing, Roseville, California, in 2001.

Printed in the United States of America

Interior illustrations by Kate Vasseur

Library of Congress Cataloging-in-Publication Data
Shaw, Kim.
    The new book of wedding etiquette : how to combine the best traditions with today's flair / Kim Shaw
        p.   cm.
    Includes index.
    1. Wedding etiquette. I. Title.
    BJ2051.W52   2000
    395.2'2—dc21   00-045640

ISBN 0-7615-2541-6

10 9 8 7 6 5 4
First Edition

For Rohan

CONTENTS

ACKNOWLEDGMENTS

I WOULD LIKE TO THANK my husband, Rohan, without whose constant encouragement and support this book would not exist. Thank you, my sweet, for listening to so many lengthy wedding monologues—you probably know more than I do by now. Thank you to my sister, Savannah, the best proofreader ever, for your unwavering faith. Thanks to my brother, Winston, for believing in this project (if the Porsche isn't delivered by next Friday, call me). Thank you to Kate Vasseur (for your wonderful illustrations as well) and Mike Kenerly—the first ones to know and to all the good karma that came from September 2, 2000. Thanks to Sarah Achenbach, for giving me *Vogue's Book of Etiquette* in 1986, and to Morrison Giffen for all your advice and encouragement.

To everyone at Something Classic Catering, many thanks for teaching me what off-site catering is all about. To Stephanie Chesson, Diane Hughes, and Deborah Triplett, photographers, thank you so much for sharing your beautiful work with me. Thanks to Cathy Freelin at East Coast Entertainment, for sisterhood and little doses of sanity. To Carolyn Shepard Design Group, thanks for all your help on the "Flowers" chapter and for always being ever so fabulous.

Finally, thank you to all my clients—past, present, and future—for allowing me to do what I love.

INTRODUCTION

Etiquette is defined as conventional requirements regarding social behavior as established in any class or community or for any occasion. This broad characterization doesn't address specifics needed by those planning a wedding, such as whether dyed-to-match bridesmaids' shoes are more correct than nice strappy black sandals, or what the proper wording for a formal invitation is, or how to exclude your second cousin's freeloading boyfriend from the guest list. Fortunately, you have chosen *The New Book of Wedding Etiquette* to answer the above questions and more, a planning strategy that's a great deal more prudent than buying a collection of etiquette books weighing as much as a cinder block.

My first word of advice to you is relax. There are few absolutes in wedding planning. Etiquette evolves; traditions begin as well as phase out. And when absolute answers aren't available, good taste will guide you to the proper choice. The etiquette police will neither speed over on motorbikes to make white-gloved arrests at your reception, nor will they crash your rehearsal dinner and edit the toasts. As a bride or groom, however, your behavior will be under greater scrutiny, and you are likely to receive more unsolicited and often misleading advice, than at any other time of your life (except, of course, when you have young children!).

Besides knowing your wedding will be done properly, there's another benefit to your reading this book. Weddings planned by those interested in adhering to proper etiquette run more smoothly, have a greater proportion of happy guests, and, generally lead to fewer family arguments than those planned by people whose favorite catchphrases are "Who's going to notice?" and "No one cares." You should also know that you shouldn't abandon etiquette in order to have a "fun, laid-back, casual" wedding—or you may experience family members fuming over seating arrangements, guests livid because no one has bothered to write them thank-yous, and your betrothed barely speaking to you after an extremely heated cash bar debate.

This book will answer all your wedding etiquette–related questions in a refreshing, relevant way. It will also uncover outdated traditions and identify those considered timeless, as well as introduce you to more contemporary customs. In fact, insights gained from this book may suggest a modern way to fulfill the traditional requirement of "something old, something new."

In 1986, a college friend bought me a wonderful old book of etiquette published in 1948. It entertained me thoroughly with advice about everything from smoking in the street to chaperoned dates to attending prizefights. Reading this book spawned my fascination with etiquette, and led to my purchasing more etiquette books published in previous and subsequent decades. I became interested in not only the changing face of etiquette, but in the perseverance of certain traditions considered proper. A corporate event planner for many years, I began my own wedding planning firm in 1998. Since then my knowledge of etiquette has been put to good use advising brides and their friends and families. I constantly deal with ordinary wedding etiquette questions ("How do I word the invitations when my parents are divorced?"), as well as more complex ones ("Should I invite a gay couple who aren't 'out'?").

Unfortunately, I also see, first hand, what happens when simple rules of etiquette are not followed, or when people feel that one of the many imaginary rules of etiquette has been breached. Hurt feelings and slighted egos are often the result when etiquette is ignored. This book is designed to help you prevent such unfortunate situations.

About the Book

THE *New Book of Wedding Etiquette* is organized to deal with etiquette issues as you are likely to encounter them during your wedding planning. The chronological arrangement encourages you to successfully clear one etiquette hurdle before you encounter the next. For instance, deciding what to wear is pointless until you've set the date. Designed to be the one etiquette book you'll need, *The New Book of Wedding Etiquette* addresses only issues relevant to decorum. For instance, here you'll find out who correctly pays for the honeymoon but will have to search elsewhere for information on how to get a passport.

You'll also benefit from reading personal reflections from brides and grooms who share real-life experiences, as well as from question-and-answer sections that expand on specific points of etiquette. The customs and traditions sidebars will give you insight into the shifty trends of propriety.

This book is intended not just for the bride and groom. Parents, who may have planned their own weddings, will nonetheless want to be up to speed for their son's or daughter's. Attendants, as participants in not only the big day but in festivities leading up to it, will also want to review this book to learn what is and what is not expected of them. Friends and family—anyone who's ever been, or ever will be, a guest at a wedding—will find helpful guest etiquette sections included in every chapter.

I hope you enjoy this book and that it helps you create a wedding day every bit as lovely as the one you've imagined.

RULES OF ENGAGEMENT

ETIQUETTE FOR THE BETROTHED

GETTING ENGAGED is one of the most exciting times of your life, and telling your friends and family the wonderful news is a real treat. Getting off on the right foot is essential; the decisions you make during the first month of your engagement are enormously important and can have long-lasting repercussions. This chapter will help you navigate your engagement smoothly, from buying the ring to writing the newspaper announcement.

The Ring and Other Engagement Presents

Two and a half million couples become engaged every year in the United States, and almost 70% of brides receive a diamond engagement ring. This ring is worn throughout the engagement on the bride's third finger of her left hand. Buying an engagement ring requires a certain level of expertise, and an effort should be made to obtain appropriate guidance. Wise grooms do not begin their education

<hr>

Dos & Don'ts

ℜ

Do set a budget prior to ring shopping.

Do buy the ring you can afford.

Do educate yourself about diamond buying.

Do consider durability when selecting a colored gemstone.

Do call the bride's parents first.

Do have the bride's family call and meet with the groom's family as soon as possible.

Don't ask or allow the bride to pay for part of the ring.

Don't buy a ring on credit terms that last longer than your engagement.

Don't reuse your old engagement ring if you're getting engaged for the second time.

<hr>

in a jeweler's showroom, at the hands of a salesperson who works on commission.

THE BUDGET

As with other aspects of your wedding, it is essential that you set a realistic budget prior to shopping for a ring. The two-month's salary rule is a popular guideline, but shouldn't be thought of as the absolute standard. The principle that applies here is that the groom pays for the ring. That does not mean purchasing a ring on credit terms that take longer than the period of engagement to reconcile. Brides may not chip in for the ring—they may, however, offer monies earmarked toward some other related expense, the honeymoon for instance, in order to free up more of the groom's capital. Although it is traditional for the ring to be presented at the time of engagement,

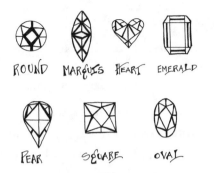

Figure 1. Seven diamond shapes.

many grooms wait to purchase the ring in order that the bride may select it herself. If you do chose to take this route, the groom should visit his jeweler first, let him or her know the budget, and make an appointment to bring his fiancée. The jeweler will then be able to show the groom's fiancée only those rings in the appropriate price range.

SETTINGS AND SHAPES

Generally speaking there are seven diamond shapes: round brilliant-cut, marquis, heart-shaped, emerald-cut, pear-shaped, square, and oval (see examples in figure 1). The round, brilliant-cut stone is far and away the most popular shape, and a stone of this shape, in a prong setting, epitomizes the traditional engagement ring. Diamonds may be set in white or yellow gold, or platinum. Styles of settings vary endlessly, the loveliest being a matter of personal taste. Gentlemen on the verge of engagement may use any number of investigative techniques in order to ascertain which settings his bride-to-be is most fond of. Depending on whom the groom consults for information (a best friend unable to keep secrets, for instance), a great deal of the "when?" surprise will be lost. A creative gentleman may make up for the disadvantage by concentrating on the where and how of the proposal.

THE FOUR CS

A diamond's value is based on four considerations: cut, carat, color, and clarity.

CUT   A well-cut or faceted diamond, regardless of its shape, reflects light and sparkle, offering the greatest brilliance and, therefore, value. Diamonds that are cut to enhance brilliance are more desirable than those cut simply to enhance carat weight. A brilliant-cut round diamond typically has fifty-seven or fifty-eight facets.

CARAT WEIGHT   Generally speaking, the larger the diamond, the rarer, and therefore the more costly. A diamond's size is measured in carat weight, and each carat is equal to 100 points. A .75 carat diamond weighs the same as a 75-point diamond or a 3/4-carat stone. Large stones are highly prized; however, their value also depends on the qualities of clarity, cut, and color. Ask your jeweler to show you stones of the same size with different values—the other three Cs will weigh in heavily to make that difference.

CLARITY   Almost all natural diamonds contain identifying characteristics; many are invisible to the naked eye. However, under a jeweler's magnifying loupe, flaws, known as inclusions, can be seen. Inclusions look like tiny crystals or clouds. Diamonds with no inclusions are categorized as flawless and are extremely rare and expensive. Diamonds with the smallest inclusions are graded as VVS1 or VVS2. The larger the inclusion, the lower the grade and the less rare the diamond. Inclusions visible to the naked eye are graded I1 or I3.

Timeless Traditions

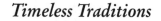

The tradition of giving a diamond engagement ring as a promise for marriage began in 1477 with the ring that Archduke Maximilian of Austria gave to Mary of Burgundy.

COLOR Pureness of color increases a diamond's rarity. Absolutely colorless stones are graded as D; lesser stones are graded continuing through the alphabet. Diamonds graded as "fancy" may be red, pink, blue, green, or canary yellow; these stones are especially rare, and therefore very valuable.

❦

THE loveliest ring will combine the very best of the four Cs that you are able to afford. A reputable jeweler will be a member of the American Gem Society or the Jewelers of America. A good jeweler will allow you to have a ring independently appraised as a requirement of the sale and once the ring has been purchased, you should have it insured for the appraised amount.

WEDDING BANDS

The wedding band may be purchased at the same time as the engagement ring, or you can wait until after you're engaged and your fiancée can choose it herself. The bride pays for the groom's ring, which may match hers, or may not, depending on the groom's taste. The wedding bands may be engraved with the couple's initials and wedding date, or, room permitting, with whatever you'd like.

HEIRLOOM RINGS

If the groom has inherited or has been given a family ring, he may present it to his fiancée as an engagement ring. He may choose to have the stone or stones reset into a more modern design, or present it unamended in order that the bride can choose the new setting. A ring returned by a past fiancée is not given to the current candidate. The groom may, however, sell such a ring and apply the proceeds toward the purchase of a new one.

The Mohs Scale

🖋

The Mohs scale of hardness was developed by Friedrich Mohs and measures the hardness of rock on a scale of 1 to 10:

1: talc	6: orthoclase
2: gypsum	7: quartz
3: calcite	8: topaz
4: flourite	9: corundum
5: apatite	10: diamond

OTHER STONES

Although a diamond is considered the most traditional of all engagement-ring stones, there is absolutely no reason to count out other stones when selecting a ring. Diamonds, however, are the hardest clear substance known to man, rating 10 on the Mohs scale (see sidebar above) of 1 to 10, and thought must be given to the hardiness of colored stones if the bride plans to wear the ring daily. Emeralds, for instance, are less durable gemstones with a hardness rating of 7.5 to 8 on the Mohs scale of 1 to 10. Emeralds with many inclusions, which are not uncommon, should be treated with care and be protected from blows. Sapphire is the gem-quality form of the mineral corundum, a crystalline form of aluminum oxide, which is one of the most durable of all minerals. With a hardness rating of 9, sapphires are well-suited for rings intended to be worn daily. Rubies, which are simply red sapphires, share the same

Birthstones

🐦

You may wish to include your fiancée's birthstone in her engagement ring. The following is the list recognized by the Jewelers of America.

January
   Color: Dark Red
   Stone: Garnet

February
   Color: Purple
   Stone: Amethyst

March
   Color: Pale Blue
   Stone: Aquamarine

April
   Color: White or Clear
   Stone: Diamond

May
   Color: Bright Green
   Stone: Emerald

June
   Color: Cream
   Stone: Moonstone

July
   Color: Red
   Stone: Ruby

August
   Color: Pale Green
   Stone: Peridot

September
   Color: Sapphire
   Stone: Deep Blue

October
   Color: Variegated
   Stone: Opal or Tourmaline

November
   Color: Yellow
   Stone: Topaz or Citrine

December
   Color: Sky Blue
   Stone: Turquoise or Blue Topaz

durability rating and are also suited to an everyday ring. A jeweler can assist you in selecting a quality stone and setting that ensures the longevity essential to an engagement ring.

OTHER ENGAGEMENT PRESENTS

Not all brides want engagement rings—and it is perfectly correct for the groom to purchase for his betrothed any present he feels she would enjoy most. Other jewelry may be popular, earrings or a necklace for instance, or one can move away from jewelry all together. My engagement "ring" for instance was a sixteen-foot red canoe. It is also correct, although not necessary, for the bride to present the groom with any present she feels he'd like, from cufflinks to cars.

Announcing the Engagement

THE next best thing to accepting a marriage proposal is announcing your engagement. Whether you choose to announce it to your friends at a surprise get-together or you call everyone just moments after you accept, take into consideration (thereby avoiding hurt feelings) those who should be the first to know.

TELLING THE PARENTS

With a first marriage, it is customary to inform the bride's parents first and, if at all possible, in person. In the event that the bride's fiancé has not yet met her parents, every effort should be made for an introduction *prior* to the announcement. Parents often aren't keen about their daughter's marrying someone they've never met. After such a meeting has been accomplished, the bride can announce the engagement to her parents as soon as she likes, even if that means calling them the moment she gets home. Although it is no longer customary, or required, a groom may certainly visit a bride's parents, or more usually, her father, in order to obtain approval and permission to marry. If this is done today, it is seen as a sweet formality, rather than a compulsory exercise, and the groom probably needn't bring along his portfolio. The bride's parents, however, do have the right to speak to the groom concerning his finances. This is particularly true if the bride is very young and may not be settled into a career or if she lives with her parents. Grooms who are marrying ladies long independent from their parents will probably be met by prospective in-laws with more relief than inquisitiveness.

The groom's parents are informed next, again, in person, and after a personal introduction. If distance prohibits a face-to-face announcement, both sets of parents may be given the news over the telephone. Requests from parents to "come and visit as soon as you can" should be anticipated and not met with "oh, I just won't have the time since I'll be taking three weeks for the honeymoon." Friends and other family members are also told as soon as convenient, again, in person if possible, or if necessary, via telephone. Letters are appropriate—not, however, ones transmitted via e-mail.

INTRODUCING THE FAMILIES

Once all sides have been informed of the wonderful news, it is essential that the groom's family contact the bride's. An arrangement to meet should be made just as quickly as possible, even if plane tickets are involved. The first meeting between parents typically includes conversation about the virtues of each of the betrothed, including the requisite childhood stories, often in conjunction with embarrassing photographs. Delaying the meeting until you are already in the throes of wedding planning is a mistake because the meeting will probably be overshadowed by conversations centering around the division of the guest list and the subsequent discussion of money. This is generally not how relationships between in-laws start out on the right foot. If for some reason (other than that they disapprove of the bride) the groom's family drags their feet about the first meeting, it is quite all right for the bride's family to make first contact.

WHEN PARENTS DISAPPROVE

Parents should take time to reflect deeply upon the reasons for their disapproval. The more valid the reason, a criminal history, for instance, the more likely that their son or daughter will need a parent's advice and support during what promises to be a challenging marriage. Religious or cultural differences are a valid reason for misgivings; however, parents should be long-sighted and think of the possibility of grandchildren before irreparably damaging their relationship with their son or daughter. The engaged couple should explain to the non-disapproving parents the source of the objection, but they should resist the urge to portray the disapproving parents in a poor light. When, hopefully, the situation is resolved, this will give the converted parents the opportunity to start over on a level playing field. Sons and daughters whose parents refuse to be swayed have no choice but to either break their engagements or continue them without their parents' approval. Those with large fortunes at stake have traditionally found the latter to be difficult, although not impossible. Please see chapter 2 for advice on the perennial favorite "I won't pay for/attend the wedding if your mother/father attends."

THE PREGNANT BRIDE

The pregnant bride is a lot more routine than many people would like to admit, a situation surely dating back to the beginning of time. Unlike in years gone by, when such scenarios were regarded as shameful, parents nowadays are likely to be pleased by the upcoming wedding, simply because many modern couples with children feel that marriage is an optional step, whereas many parents feel the two go hand in hand. Even though parents may well make a huge fuss about it to start with, they're usually won over by the birth of the adorable grandchild. The pregnant bride goes about her business in the same manner as any other bride and pretends not to hear silly questions such as "Well if you weren't, would you still be getting married?" and any other tiresome remarks uttered by friends and family alike. The bride and groom should plan the wedding around the birth, and accomplish the nuptials soon enough to be convenient. No bride wants to get married while nine-months pregnant, even if it is the first Saturday in June. Brides may not move the wedding date until after the birth date "So I'll be able to drink and have a good time." She and the groom may certainly host a marriage celebration after their wedding and the birth of their child if a party is high on their list of priorities. If for whatever reason the wedding cannot be scheduled until after the birth (the groom's proposal in the delivery room for instance) then the wedding may take place after the bride is fully recovered. Baby showers may be combined into wedding showers, and the couple's wedding gift registry may include whatever baby-related items they require. There is no special etiquette regarding a pregnant bride's attire, as long as whatever she's wearing fits properly.

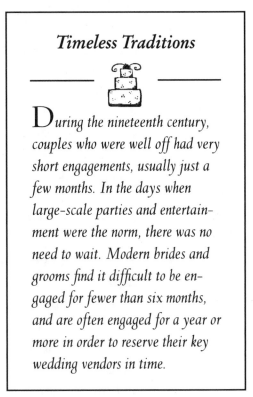

Timeless Traditions

During the nineteenth century, couples who were well off had very short engagements, usually just a few months. In the days when large-scale parties and entertainment were the norm, there was no need to wait. Modern brides and grooms find it difficult to be engaged for fewer than six months, and are often engaged for a year or more in order to reserve their key wedding vendors in time.

Engagement for the Second Marriage

BEING engaged for a second (or third, or fourth) time subjects one to a few rules that do not apply to those engaged for the first time. The first and foremost rule is that no one can be married and also engaged, and no one can be engaged to someone already married. This applies to everyone, including those who are "expecting the paperwork any day now" or who have been "separated for years" and are just waiting for the "formalities." No matter what promises have been made, or how a couple may have set up housekeeping, there can be no public talk of engagement, or wearing of an engagement ring until divorces are final, and all bets, so to speak, are off. Ladies who receive three-carat diamond rings from gentlemen not (exactly) estranged from their wives, have not received an engagement ring and may not refer to it as such.

Divorced ladies do not wear their previous engagement ring, nor do they recycle their wedding bands. They may, however, have the stones from either or both rings set into another piece of jewelry. Divorced gentlemen do not recycle their wedding bands either. Widowed persons do not continue to wear their wedding bands and engagement rings from their prior marriage. The engagement ring may be saved as an heirloom or the stones set into another piece of jewelry.

TELLING THE EX-SPOUSE

Generally the first person divorced individuals should inform of their impending nuptials is the ex-husband or wife. This of course is logical if you have children together and you parted with a handshake and "Good luck!" If you have no children and your last words were more along the lines of "I'll see you in hell," then you may forgo this step and move right along with telling your parents in the manner described above.

TELLING THE CHILDREN

If either of you have children from a previous marriage or relationship, it is essential that they be told second, after telling your ex-spouse. It's sensible to let children warm up to the idea, so don't just spring it on them, especially if they are close to the ex-husband or wife. If both of you have children and your households will combine, the children will need quite a while to get used to new siblings as well as a new stepparent, so be prepared. It's good to keep in mind during the adjustment period that *The Brady Bunch* was only a TV show. If you are widowed and have grown children, it is also appropriate to let them know first. See chapter 4 for advice on including your children in your wedding.

Printed Engagement Announcements

PRINTED engagement announcements appear in the newspapers of the bride and groom's hometown, and in each of their parents' hometowns if everyone lives in a different place. The announcement may appear along with a photograph of the bride or with one of the bride and groom. Most newspapers will provide you with a form to fill out, but announcements correctly include particular information. See the following example:

> *Mr. and Mrs. Harold James Phillips of Beaufort, South Carolina announce the engagement of their daughter Miss Julia Helen Phillips to Mr. John Christopher Haysworth, son of Mr. and Mrs. Charles Edward Haysworth of Richmond, Virginia. A June wedding is planned.*
>
> *Miss Phillips is a graduate of Hollins University and is a high school teacher for Henrico County Public Schools in Richmond, Virginia. Mr. Haysworth is a graduate of Davidson College and the University of Virginia School of Law and is an attorney for the law firm of Johnson and Haysworth in Richmond, Virginia.*

One need not be so specific as to the date: "A summer wedding is planned" is also correct. Also, "Ms." may be substituted for "Miss" in all scenarios.

WHEN A PARENT IS DECEASED

The wording is different when paying respect to a deceased parent. Following are examples of each scenario:

WHEN THE BRIDE'S MOTHER IS DECEASED

Mr. Harold James Phillips of Beaufort, South Carolina announces the engagement of his daughter, Miss Julia Helen Phillips to Mr. John Christopher Haysworth, son of Mr. and Mrs. Charles Edward Haysworth, of Richmond, Virginia. Miss Phillips is also the daughter of the late Susan Laura Phillips.

WHEN THE BRIDE'S FATHER IS DECEASED

Mrs. Harold James Phillips of Beaufort, South Carolina announces the engagement of her daughter, Miss Julia Helen Phillips to Mr. John Christopher Haysworth, son of Mr. and Mrs. Charles Edward Haysworth, of Richmond, Virginia. Miss Phillips is also the daughter of the late Harold James Phillips.

WHEN BOTH OF THE BRIDE'S PARENTS ARE DECEASED

The bride's godparents or closest relative may issue the announcement, or the bride herself may issue it in the third person.

Mr. and Mrs. Spencer Lee Phillips of Beaufort, South Carolina, announce the engagement of his sister, Miss Julia Helen Phillips, daughter of the late Mr. and Mrs. Harold James Phillips, to Mr. John Christopher Haysworth, son of Mr. and Mrs. Charles Edward Haysworth, of Richmond, Virginia.

OR

The engagement of Miss Julia Helen Phillips, daughter of the late Mr. and Mrs. Harold James Phillips, is announced, to Mr. John Christopher Haysworth . . .

WHEN THE GROOM'S MOTHER IS DECEASED

Mr. and Mrs. Harold James Phillips of Beaufort, South Carolina announce the engagement of their daughter, Miss Julia Helen Phillips to Mr. John Christopher

Haysworth, son of Mr. Charles Edward Haysworth, of Richmond, Virginia and the late Jane Kelly Haysworth.

WHEN THE GROOM'S FATHER IS DECEASED

Mr. and Mrs. Harold James Phillips of Beaufort, South Carolina announce the engagement of their daughter, Miss Julia Helen Phillips to Mr. John Christopher Haysworth, son of Mrs. Charles Edward Haysworth, of Richmond, Virginia and the late Charles Edward Haysworth.

WHEN BOTH OF THE GROOM'S PARENTS ARE DECEASED

Mr. and Mrs. Harold James Phillips of Beaufort, South Carolina, announce the engagement of their daughter, Miss Julia Helen Phillips, to Mr. John Christopher Haysworth, son of the late Mr. and Mrs. Charles Edward Haysworth . . .

WHEN THE BRIDE IS A WIDOW

If the bride is a young widow, her parents may announce her engagement in the same manner as the first time, only they use her current name:

Mr. and Mrs. Harold James Phillips of Beaufort, South Carolina, announce the engagement of their daughter, Mrs. Alan Derrick Reynolds, to Mr. John Christopher Haysworth, son of Mr. and Mrs. Charles Edward Haysworth . . .

If the bride is an older widow, she announces the engagement in the third person:

The engagement of Mrs. Steven Ashton Pierce, daughter of (or the late if they are deceased) Mr. and Mrs. Harold James Phillips, is announced, to Mr. John Christopher Haysworth . . .

WHEN THE BRIDE IS DIVORCED

The bride may announce the engagement in the third person, or her parents may issue the announcement (usual in the case of a young divorcee).

The engagement of Mrs. Julia Davis (or Julia Phillips Davis), *daughter of Mr. and Mrs. Harold James Phillips, is announced, to Mr. John Christopher Haysworth . . .*

OR

Mr. and Mrs. Harold James Phillips of Beaufort, South Carolina, announce the engagement of their daughter, Mrs. Julia Davis (or Julia Phillips Davis), *to Mr. John Christopher Haysworth, son of Mr. and Mrs. Charles Edward Haysworth . . .*

WHEN THE BRIDE'S PARENTS ARE DIVORCED

When the bride's mother has not remarried:

Mrs. (or Ms.) *Susan Laura Phillips* (or Susan Andrews Phillips, Andrews being her maiden name) *of Beaufort, South Carolina, announces the engagement of her daughter, Miss Julia Helen Phillips . . . Miss Phillips is also the daughter of Mr. Harold James Phillips . . .*

When the bride's mother has remarried:

Mrs. James Patrick Howard of Ardmore, Pennsylvania, announces the engagement of her daughter, Miss Julia Helen Phillips . . . Miss Phillips is also the daughter of Mr. Harold James Phillips . . .

If the bride's mother has remarried and the divorce is a rather more friendly one:

Mrs. James Patrick Howard, of Ardmore, Pennsylvania, and Mr. Harold James Phillips of Beaufort, South Carolina, announce the engagement of their daughter, Miss Julia Helen Phillips . . .

If both parents have remarried and everyone is friendly:

Mr. and Mrs. James Patrick Howard, of Ardmore, Pennsylvania, and Mr. and Mrs. Harold James Phillips of Beaufort, South Carolina, announce the engagement of Mrs. Howard's and Mr. Phillips's daughter, Miss Julia Helen Phillips . . .

WHEN THE GROOM'S PARENTS ARE DIVORCED

When the groom's mother has not remarried:

Mr. and Mrs. Harold James Phillips of Beaufort, South Carolina, announce the engagement of their daughter, Miss Julia Helen Phillips, to Mr. John Christopher Haysworth, son of Mrs. (or Ms.) *Jane Kelly Haysworth* (or Jane Fischer Haysworth, Fischer being her maiden name), *of Richmond, Virginia, and Mr. Charles Edward Haysworth . . .*

When the groom's mother has remarried:

Mr. and Mrs. Harold James Phillips of Beaufort, South Carolina, announce the engagement of their daughter, Miss Julia Helen Phillips, to Mr. John Christopher Haysworth, son of Mrs. Franklin Peter Hughes of Chevy Chase, Maryland, and Mr. Charles Edward Haysworth . . .

If both the groom's parents have remarried and everyone is friendly:

Mr. and Mrs. Harold James Phillips of Beaufort, South Carolina, announce the engagement of their daughter, Miss Julia Helen Phillips, to Mr. John Christopher Haysworth, son of Mr. and Mrs. Franklin Peter Hughes of Chevy Chase, Maryland, and Mr. and Mrs. Charles Edward Haysworth . . .

WHEN THE COUPLE ANNOUNCES THEIR OWN ENGAGEMENT

Unless there's a really good reason for this—for instance, older couples, especially when all parents are deceased, or much-divorced couples—this route tends to look as if the bride's parents don't approve of the match.

Miss Julia Helen Phillips and Mr. John Christopher Haysworth are pleased to announce their engagement . . .

The Broken Engagement

In the event of a broken engagement, a statement should be sent to the same newspaper(s) that carried the engagement announcement.

The engagement of Miss Julia Helen Phillips and Mr. John Christopher Haysworth has been broken by mutual consent.

Even if that's not true, the real reason, no doubt, is not fit to print.

RETURNING GIFTS

In the case of a broken engagement any engagement or wedding gifts must be returned with a short note.

Dear Fiona,

I'm really sorry to let you know that John and I have broken our engagement. I'm returning the martini glasses that you were so sweet to send to me.

Love,
Julia

Engagement Parties

ANYONE who chooses may throw an engagement party; if the bride and groom would like to surprise their friends with their announcement, they may throw a party themselves under some other guise. For example, they could host a get-together for Cinco de Mayo or another holiday and make the announcement then. Family and close friends of the principals involved are invited, and the guest list may be as limited as the host chooses. For instance, if the bride's old college roommate is hostess, she may invite the bride and groom's parents, siblings, and the bride's college friends only. Persons invited to an engagement party may or may not be invited to the wedding. The host's "really hilarious" neighbors, invited as a courtesy, but complete strangers to the couple and their families, need not be invited to the wedding. Gifts are not a requirement at an engagement party, and no indication should be given that they are. Since not everyone will bring a gift, the bride and groom should refrain from opening any they do receive during the party. Toasting may certainly be done by whoever thinks himself eloquent. Invitations may be sent via post, telephone, or e-mail. Prompt thankyou letters must be written by the bride and groom to their hosts, as well as to any guests who gave gifts.

Who Pays for What in the Event of a Broken Engagement?

&

My ex-fiancé and I were engaged for four months, until, two months prior to the wedding, he broke the engagement. Aside from this being just an awful and embarrassing situation, my parents and I are out quite a bit of money. We'd already put down deposits with the caterer, the photographer, a band, a site, a florist, plus we had the invitations. My question is this: What does my ex-fiancé have to pay for? If he won't pay, do I have the right to sell the ring and use it to offset the expenses?

A broken engagement is indeed an awful, sad, and embarrassing situation— all the more reason to resist the temptation to make it even more awful, sad, and embarrassing. This is a matter of highly charged emotions and hurt feelings and is not quite the same as entering into a dispute with the gentleman one had retained to rebuild one's carburetor. Since you say that you and your parents are out of pocket, I imagine that you were involved in planning a traditional wedding, reliant on the bride's family's shouldering most of the cost. Unfortunately, your family is also going to have to shoulder the loss of nonrefundable deposits. You may, however, attempt to renegotiate contracts to your advantage. While a caterer may not refund your deposit for a cancellation, I'm quite certain that they would be happy, with two months notice, to change the date of your event. That is to say, instead of losing your deposit, allow the caterer to hold on to the monies until such time as you or your parents feel like having a party. I realize that entertaining is not your priority now, but that may well change. You must promise, however, not to sulk about the party, assaulting guests with such remarks as "You know, this was going to be my wedding crab dip." You may try this "not now, later" approach where practical, in order to hang onto as many deposits as possible.

If one could put aside one's anger long enough, one should consider saving the envelopes/reply cards from the invitations, should there be a need, in the future, to purchase invitations of the exact same type for a similar event. You may, of course, ask your ex-fiancé to assist you and your parents with offsetting expenses, however, if he does not wish to avail himself of the opportunity, you may not, under any circumstances, sell the ring and use the proceeds to pay off florists or what have you. The ring is given as a promise to marry, when that promise is broken (technically always by the lady, inquires directed to the gentleman are answered with "it was really all my fault"——no elaboration is allowed), the ring is returned. No doubt, many of your caring friends have already pointed out "Well thank goodness it happened now, and we're just talking about a caterer, not alimony and custody." This is supposed to afford you some consolation, unfortunately, all such sentiments ("Hey, think of it this way, next time you'll be a pro at wedding planning!") cannot help but sound crass and well-meaning friends should attempt to avoid them. A simple "I know you're going to be so much happier this way" and an invitation to lunch is better.

Etiquette for Friends and Guests

FRIENDS of engaged couples will kindly refrain from such comments as "That's a really big ring, is it real?" or "Wow! How much did that set you back?" If the engaged lady does not have an engagement ring, it's really not nice, unless the lady is involved in some activity that would cause her to lose her ring, to pick up her hand in astonishment and blurt "Where's your ring?" Friends try to be supportive of the couple and do not launch into wedding-planning horror stories such as "I swear, I thought Tom and I were going to break up over the catering," or make sly comments that include phrases such as "ball and chain." Friends also do not enlighten the bride and groom with statistics concerning the current rate of divorce. "Friends" who feel compelled to ask questions such as "Am I going to be invited to the wedding?" probably won't be. Friends who have something helpful to say—"Thelma and I've been married going on forty years now"—should speak up.

Guests at engagement parties may bring gifts if they choose, but they don't embarrass the bride and groom and other guests by insisting "Open it! Open it!" all evening.

Wedding Day Reflections

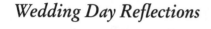

When we got engaged, my fiancé bought me a plain white gold band as an engagement present— exactly what I wanted. Almost every time people said, "let me see the ring," and I extended my hand, they would twist the ring around in order to find the stone. It was really embarrassing, for me as well as them.

—Kate

2

BANK ON IT

Etiquette and Money

THE ASPECT OF wedding planning with the least potential for delight, the frank discussion of money, must take place just as soon as possible. This chapter will guide you through some sticky etiquette points that invariably surround money matters—from how to ask for money to how to accept it (and refuse it). Money withheld as a bribe or given with strings attached is also addressed. Just keep in mind, that once you're over this hurdle, the real fun of wedding planning can begin.

Who Pays for What?

WHETHER the bride's family pays for almost everything, or the wedding budget is a combination of resources, it is absolutely essential to establish a budget before moving forward with any aspect of planning.

PARENTS

Chances are (hopefully), both sets of parents are very excited for this day, and will be delighted to cover most, if not all, of the costs. But you should know what to ask for so you don't cross the line or step on anyone's toes.

THE BRIDE'S PARENTS   Traditionally, the bride's parents paid for practically everything, and it was considered a breech of etiquette for the groom's family to pay for anything, although the groom had a few financial responsibilities. The bride's family hosted a wedding in keeping with their financial situation, and the relative wealth or poverty of the groom had nothing to do with the grandness of the wedding. A girl from a poor family who married a millionaire had a wedding in the style of her parents, however meager their resources. Nowadays, it is very common to see brides and grooms paying for their own weddings, with little or no help from their parents. It is also common to see both sets of parents, not just the bride's, chip in as well. Wedding budgets now involve more people than ever, not just the bride's father, so you must establish who will be paying, and how much, before proceeding with any other aspect of your planning. Early on, a meeting should be arranged with the principals in order to ascertain what the bride's parents are willing to contribute and what

---

Wedding Day Reflections

When I got engaged, I had an absolute vision of what I wanted, but I had no idea of the costs. My parents are divorced so they offered to pay for specific things: my mom, for instance, said she'd pay for the catering and the band, and my dad said he'd pay for the flowers, the rentals, and the transportation. Of course, the dollar amounts didn't add up equally and they ended up arguing about the money, and putting me in the middle. Finally, I went with a compromise that was not as costly, but nothing even close to the wedding and reception I'd envisioned. If I had to do it all again, I'd have had a budget in mind and would have asked them to give whatever percentage they felt they could afford.

—Tez

the engaged couple may have to offer as well. It is doubtful that parents will come across with an arbitrary sum, so it's a good idea to do a little research and ask for an actual dollar amount. Wedding professionals in your area are a good resource, wedding planners, catering-event planners, and banquet managers can all give you at least a ballpark figure on the cost of weddings in your city. You should also ascertain how many guests you and your respective parents will be inviting—there's an obvious difference in cost between a reception for 300 guests and one for 100. Parents will also want to know how much money you need right away and how much you'll need closer to the wedding day or on the day itself. Again, wedding professionals in your area will be able to give you an estimate for up-front deposit amounts. It is also a good idea, especially if parents don't live in the same city as the bride and groom or in the city where the wedding will take place, for the couple to set up a separate wedding expense account and have parents make their deposit(s) directly. This way, the couple can pay vendors themselves and keep track of their expenditures accurately.

THE GROOM'S PARENTS   If the bride and groom have been engaged for ages, or if they're from the same small town, it's likely that both sets of parents know one another and one another's financial situations fairly well. In this case, it is not improper for the groom's parents to offer to contribute to the overall budget early in the process. Great tact must be demonstrated in doing so, usually excuses like "Because we have so many more relatives than you" or "With ten partners at the office, it is going to be terrible trying to keep Stan's side of the guest list down" are offered. The impression that the groom's parents are contributing in order to accomplish a wedding more to their taste than the bride's parents' will probably start a family feud that will last at least as long their son's marriage. Beware that hostilities of this type pick up further momentum when grandchildren come into the picture and that altercations between grandparents concerning the elaborateness of

Christmas presents, and later, funding for college educations, tend to keep bitter grudges as good as new. In any case, the parents of the bride may accept the money offered to them or they may politely refuse it. In the case of a refusal, the groom's parents consider the decision as final and don't try to make back-door contributions by "paying for the bar as a wedding present" and so forth. The bride and groom also realize the decision is final and do not attempt to pressure her parents into accepting because they'd like a grander reception. If the groom's parents do not know the bride's parents well, or at all, they should exercise caution when it comes to offering money, and should wait to be approached by the couple or her family. This is doubly true if the groom's family is considerably wealthier than the bride's. The unsolicited offer of a great deal of money, especially right off the bat, is likely to be seen by the bride's family as an insult to their limited means, rather than a good deed designed to enhance the wedding.

Strictly as a matter of etiquette, keep in mind that the groom's parents are under no obligation to pay for anything. While it is usual for them to host a rehearsal dinner the evening prior to the wedding, it is not required and the dinner itself is a relatively new custom, not subject to any special rule of fiscal etiquette. This does not, however, mean that the bride gets her way on everything "Because my parents are paying for everything and yours are just having the rehearsal dinner." See the section in this chapter called "Here Comes the Bribe" for more information on principals throwing their weight around because they've paid more.

WHEN PARENTS CAN'T OR WON'T PAY (FOR MUCH)

It is unwise to assume that parents have been squirreling away money for years and years in order to pay for your wedding and reception. If the bride's family refuses to pay for anything, one must immediately ascertain whether or not they can't or simply won't pay. (See the "Here Comes the Bribe" section of this chapter for further insights into "won't.") If the bride's parents genuinely cannot afford to contribute to the wedding, the couple may approach the groom's parents, without encouraging them to speculate whether or not lack of funding from the bride's family comes from genuine financial embarrassment or just plain meanness. (Remember that you'll be married forever and that making trouble between your in-laws isn't going to make your union any happier.) If the groom's family cannot provide assistance, the couple has no choice but to move forward with paying for their own wedding. In any case, unless the parents actually disapprove of the bride or groom (see chapter 1), it's probably unlikely that they're actually trying to make a statement by not funding the wedding. If parents can't afford to pay for much, but still are willing to offer a little, the bride and groom can consider a wedding budget based on a combination of resources. Regardless of what tactics you may believe are underway, monies, even in an amount that doesn't measure up to your idea of a sufficient contribution, must be accepted graciously.

WHEN PARENTS ARE DIVORCED   If either or both sets of the couple's parents are divorced, even greater diplomacy must be employed when asking for money. Unless relationships are extremely friendly, divorced parents should be approached separately. Inevitably, the question "How much is your father/mother giving?" will come up. This is a difficult question to answer, especially if parents' resources are considerably different. It may work a little better to answer in terms of a percentage: "Well, Dad says he can give around 40% of our total budget, which is going to be around $20,000." It may be easier for a parent to answer with "Well then, I'll give 30%" rather than having to come up with a matching dollar amount. Divorced parents should not consider budget talks a golden opportunity to revisit the financial conflicts that distinguished their marriage, estrangement, and divorce.

Divorced Parents and Money

❧

I have recently become engaged, and the games, it seems, have already begun. My parents divorced five years ago and my father remarried soon after. My mother, however, remains single. She is going to pay for the entire wedding, but has already indicated to me that if I invite my father and his wife, she won't pay for a thing. Although I wasn't planning on having him walk me down the aisle, I would like my father, who I love, and his wife, who I've grown close to over the years, to attend. My fiancé and I can't afford the kind of wedding we'd like on our own, so this is really quite a predicament. Could I just invite my father and his wife without telling my mother? By the time she sees them, it will be too late to change anything. I love both my parents and am really torn about making this decision.

Welcome to planning one of the most important days of your entire life. Someone's promising financial backing as an inducement for you to do something you'd rather not (such as excluding your father and his wife from your wedding), is called bribery, not wedding planning. This is for your information only—using the word "bribe" in conjunction with the word "caterer" is not going to motivate your mother in the way you might imagine. The challenge here is figuring out how to have your wedding cake and eat it, too. Do not invite your father and his wife without telling your mother; trust me, by the time she sees them, it won't be "too late to change anything." You'd be sur-

prised how quickly a day of bliss and harmony can turn into round two of a bitter divorce, complete with "no-holds-barred" action. What I suggest is this: You and your fiancé pay for your own wedding ceremony, to which you may invite whoever you please, while your mother funds the wedding reception, to which she may invite whoever she pleases. This will not be inexpensive, but certainly it beats your paying for the entire event. Your responsibilities may include, depending on your mother's frame of mind, the fee for the minister and possibly the ceremony site, the floral decorations, and any photography or videography that takes place during the ceremony plus the cost of your transportation. Your father and his wife should be sent an invitation to the ceremony, like any other guest, only without the "reception immediately following" card. I'm certain that your father is quite well-acquainted with the reason your mother is determined not to play hostess to him and his wife at the reception, and will not be surprised by the exclusion. Be prepared, however, for your mother to refuse to fork out for the reception even under these circumstances. While I sympathize with your desire to have "the kind of wedding we'd like," I tend to doubt that any amount of champagne or flowers will compensate for your deliberate omission of those you love. Therefore, you and your fiancé should brace yourselves for funding and hosting your own wedding, which will enable you to issue invitations to all feuding parties. You may then make this appeal to everyone concerned: Your engagement is not an interlude during which those who have not succeeded at what you are about to attempt may review the motivation behind their failure.

ALTERNATIVE SOURCES

You may have to pool together many financial resources besides your parents for one reason or another—don't be discouraged, just learn the most appropriate ways to handle the situation(s).

OTHER DONORS As I have already mentioned, couples are prohibited from calling relatives and complaining about the modesty of their budgets in order to raise a sympathetic few bucks. With that in mind, brides and grooms should be prepared for unsolicited offers of funds. If the bride's parents or the bride's and groom's parents are shouldering the entire responsibility, it is best to rechannel the unsolicited offer through the appropriate set of parents. In this way, parents won't be surprised and egos won't be wounded when the bride pipes up "Oh, don't worry about the extra three hors d'oeuvres selections, Uncle John's money is going to pay for it." If the bride or groom or both are paying for part or all of the wedding, they can accept the money themselves, although parents should still be made aware of the contribution. Couples should keep in mind that it is not unusual for donors to expect that money will buy a stake in planning process. Obviously, relatives who are pushy during the holidays and family get-togethers (you know the ones) aren't likely to just drop off the check and leave well enough alone. You must decide how much interference you're willing to put up with in return for the cash, because once you've accepted the money, you're likely to have to contend with this sort of thing:

> Donor relative: "But I always thought you'd have a sit-down dinner, just like your cousin Mildred's back home."

> Bride/Groom (Who hated Mildred's reception but is trying to be diplomatic): "Well, actually we really didn't want anything quite that formal, we thought a buffet might be more fun and less expensive."

Donor relative: "Sit-down is more fun—and now you have the money for it. You know Mildred had the most wonderful Cornish game hens, I can call her caterer and get the recipe . . . "

With that in mind, you may wish to turn down an offer, kindly and tactfully. By the same token, couples should realize that their own financial contribution does not entitle them to stomp all over other people's opinions either. "Well we're paying for the bar" doesn't mean that you can ignore your mother's horror over the butlered "sex on the beach" shooters.

CREDIT CARDS   There is no rule against charging the entire cost of the wedding to a credit card. There is, however, if one does not pay off the card in the proper time, a rule against complaining months or years after the wedding that "I'm still paying for it."

FUNDRAISING   Couples may not spend their engagement fundraising in an effort to shore up the wedding budget. This includes, but is not limited to, calling up relatives to complain about lack of funds in the hopes that they'll write checks, or encouraging friends to throw showers with "stock the wedding reception bar" or "chip in for the band" themes. Couples are also absolutely prohibited from passing any wedding-related expenses along to guests. That means that you are absolutely forbidden to have a cash bar at your wedding. There are no exceptions to this rule, ever.

Here Comes the Bribe

BRIBERY is not a very nice word, nor is it a complete stranger to wedding planning. Statements such as "We're not paying for a thing unless you get married in our church/synagogue" or "If he/she is coming,

(continued on page 34)

How to Save When the Bride and Groom Pay

❧

My fiancé and I have just gotten engaged and are in the begin-
ning planning stages. We've picked a date for next April, so we
have plenty of time for planning (ten months). We're going to
be paying for this wedding ourselves and needless to say, our
budget is extremely limited. What can we do to save money? We
both want a really nice reception but things like limousines and
formal portraits are way out of our league. Neither sets of par-
ents are in a position to help much, but will be attending.

A *really nice reception is one that includes the following elements:*

- *A happy and relaxed bride and groom*

- *Nonfeuding family members (if only for the day)*

- *Guests who have a genuine interest in the happiness of either the couple, or the*
  couple's parents, or any combination thereof

- *A cake*

- *A drink of some sort with which to toast the happy couple*

Providing that you comply with the above, I'm completely confident that you and
your fiancé will have "a really nice reception." In answer to your inquiry "What
can we do to save money?" I offer the following.

- Limit your guest list. *By this I don't mean excluding your parents' close*
  friends or your first cousins who live ten minutes from you so that you can
  serve full bar and rack of lamb as opposed to beer, wine, and grilled chicken.
  Invite only those close to either you or your parents and let everyone else, in-
  cluding business associates with whom you do not socialize, know that your
  wedding will be "A very small, just close family really, affair." Send unin-
  vited acquaintances, distant relatives, and family who you know cannot attend

because of distance, health, etc., a wedding announcement, mailed the day of the wedding. Uninvited guests shouldn't be expected to attend showers nor are they required to send a wedding gift.

♦ Don't have a reception that coincides with a mealtime. *Hors d'oeuvres and tea receptions are significantly less expensive than full lunches or dinners; brunch is also quite inexpensive. Also, consider serving soft drinks, beer, and wine instead of a full bar and limit champagne consumption to toasting only. Brunch, in addition to being an inexpensive meal is doubly attractive because one never need have a full bar; fresh juices, soft drinks, coffee, and mimosas are ample refreshment.*

♦ Consider holding your wedding on a Friday or Sunday. *Many venues charge as little as half the Saturday rate on these off days.*

♦ Don't schedule your wedding immediately prior to big "flower" holidays. *A few weeks before Mother's Day and Valentine's Day, demand drives up florists' prices significantly.*

♦ Don't hold your wedding on a busy weekend. *For instance, if you live in a university town, don't plan your wedding for any weekend that coincides with large sporting events held in your city or on graduation/parents' weekend. Hotel rooms will be hard to come by and at a premium.*

♦ Resist the urge to enlist a lot of friends and family into doing chores or providing services during your reception. *It is almost always disconcerting for a guest to ascertain, after a few moments at your reception, that he is one of the few who appear not to be working.*

♦ Instead of writing lots of checks for wedding expenses, use a credit card that gives you airline miles and pay it off every month. *You might just have enough for a couple of honeymoon airline tickets by the end of it.*

♦ Above all, remember that getting married and throwing a party, although not mutually exclusive, do not rate the same level of importance. *No doubt, on your ten-year wedding anniversary, you will be more likely to rejoice in having spent the decade with your wife, than reflect on the merits of the smoked salmon served at your reception.*

(continued from page 31)

I'm not paying for a thing" are not unheard of either. Parents who use financial backing as a way to encourage the bride and groom to comply with their wishes probably aren't withholding their money wisely. Compromise is key and should be applied vigorously to any differences, particularly those concerning religion. For example, in the case of a mixed marriage, it is often possible to have two officiants, one from each religion, to conduct the service and combine elements of both faiths. If the couple objects to the idea of a church wedding, rather than the minister, it is possible that the officiant from the parents' church could conduct the service at some other site. (See chapter 8 for more information on ceremonies.) The engaged couple should exhibit a great degree of flexibility also, but if dearly held principals would be violated by compromise, they should be prepared to pay for their own wedding. Divorced parents should keep in mind that dissatisfaction with their former spouse has nothing to do with their children. Threatening to pull financial backing unless an act of revenge is accomplished (one parent not being invited to the wedding, for example) does not set a good example to engaged persons.

Tipping

EARLY on you may not be able to figure out exactly how much of your budget will go to tips—you may not know, for instance, which vendors will include gratuities in the overall invoice and which don't, but you should be prepared to know who gets tipped, and roughly how much. The largest gratuity amount will be on your reception invoice. Most hotels and country clubs will include the gratuity (usually around 18%) on the total bill, but check with the hotel or club manager to see if there are any other usual gratuities not included in the bill. Off-site catering companies may or may not include a gratuity on your invoice, so check to make sure. If your catering invoice is due prior to the reception, which is not unusual, you may wish to make out a separate tip check (usually at 10% to15% of the food and liquor cost), as opposed to adding it to your total. Don't fill out the amount until during the reception; that way, you can be sure the amount reflects your approval of the service. The catering manager or catering event planner will see that the tip is distributed among servers, bartenders, and others. Because hosts, not guests, are responsible for gratuities, bartenders should not, regardless of where the reception is held, have a tip jar on the bar, nor should they solicit tips to be given to them directly.

Check your transportation invoices to see if gratuity for drivers is included, if not, you may add them to your bill, or tip in cash (15% to 20% of the total). Porters (at least $2 per bag), powder room attendants ($1 per guest), parking attendants ($2 per car) and taxi cab drivers (10% to 15% of the bill) will need to be tipped, so be sure to have the appropriate amount of cash handy on the day of the wedding. Officiants are not tipped, however, if you wish to contribute money to the church/synagogue, in addition to the regular fee, you may do so, provided your intent is clear. Wedding planners do not receive gratuities.

Timeless Traditions

T*he trousseau was the "little trusse or bundle" that the bride carried with her to her husband's house. Generally the trousseau was made up of household linens that the bride and her family had been collecting for many years, possibly since her birth, in addition to all her personal clothing, and was always part of the bride's family's financial obligation. Since the trousseau was collected long before the bridegroom's name was known, all monograms were made up of the bride's initials.*

Etiquette for Friends and Relatives

SINCE the bride, the groom, and their parents should exercise much discretion when it comes to the delicate subject of money, no one but very close friends ought to be privy to any information concerning

---

Dos & Don'ts

❧

Do figure out a ballpark budget before asking for money.

Do ask parents for money as soon as possible.

Do be grateful for whatever monies your parents provide.

Do participate in compromise if your parents feel strongly about some aspects of your wedding.

Do be aware that money is sometimes given with strings attached.

Do tip based on a job well done.

Don't start planning without knowing how much you have to spend.

Don't assume that the bride's parents are going to pay for everything.

Don't assume that the groom's parents are required to pay for anything, including a rehearsal dinner.

Don't ask friends and relatives to contribute to your budget.

Don't allow yourself to be bribed into abandoning principals.

Don't forget to carry some cash for tips on your wedding day.

---

the budget. Vendors may, but friends and relatives may not, ask the principals how much they have to spend. If friends and relatives wish to provide wedding funding, but do not wish to incur the gratitude (or wrath) of parents, they may certainly attempt to throw their hats into the ring by giving the couple money as a wedding gift. They may not, however, dictate that the funds be spent on the wedding or get huffy if it is not. Parents who are contributing money to the wedding, no matter how much, do not make a big production of it by going around telling everyone who'll listen how expensive everything is and how much the event is costing overall. Remember, one of the most serious violations of wedding etiquette is spending more than you can afford.

3

SETTING THE STAGE

Etiquette for Planning

Now that all budget discussions are (hopefully) resolved, you can get down to the business of planning your wedding. Etiquette pitfalls can be numerous in this stage of your engagement, so it's important to start things off on the right foot, because if you don't, errors tend to snowball. Queries abound now: Can an outside ceremony be formal? What constitutes an informal reception? What is the right thing to wear at what time? Does the bride's mother choose her outfit first? You will find that during this period of your engagement, relatives and friends are asking *you* the questions. This chapter will give you all the answers, as well as a sound foundation on which the rest of your wedding plans can be built.

When and Where

Set your priorities when it comes to choosing a date. Is May 21st absolutely a must because it's the same as your parents' wedding date, or is having your reception at a particular site paramount? There is no date more correct than another, although June is traditional. Keep in mind though, that Lent and Passover are considered to be solemn periods that do not lend themselves to large, festive weddings. Advent is a very busy time for Christian churches, so plan far ahead if a Christmas wedding is your priority. Being flexible about your date is essential, especially if you have less than a year to plan your wedding and reception. Try thinking in terms of an ideal season, rather than a specific day. Check carefully with your chamber of commerce to find out what upcoming events might coincide with your ideal wedding date. Sporting events, conventions, and festivals can make reception locations and hotel rooms scarce. Holidays such as Valentine's Day and Mother's Day create a high demand for flowers so expect to pay more around these holidays.

Timeless Traditions

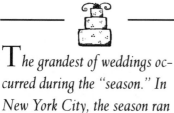

The grandest of weddings occurred during the "season." In New York City, the season ran from the opening of the Metropolitan Opera until the first day of Lent. In New Orleans, the season ran from late November until Mardi Gras, the Tuesday before Ash Wednesday.

THE DAY OF THE WEEK

Generally weddings are held on Saturdays or Sundays (Jewish weddings held on Saturdays must take place after sundown), in order to accommodate the Sabbath and work schedules. You may certainly hold your wedding on a Friday or any other day of the week, providing you give guests plenty of warning and anticipate that not as many persons as you would like will be able to attend. You are welcome to choose a weekday in order to keep your guest count down, just don't let on.

THE CEREMONY SITE

The traditional location for a wedding ceremony is a house of worship (generally the bride's or her parents'), and the most formal weddings generally take place there. When you confirm the date with your house of worship, also confirm the availability of your minister, priest, or rabbi; you also may want to hold your church for several dates until you confirm the availability of your reception site. The size of the church or synagogue is obviously a factor and you should chose a location that is able to accommodate the number of guests you anticipate attending. If you and your fiancé do not belong to a particular church, you may find that nondenominational churches and chapels, particularly those on college campuses, are able to accommodate you. You may wish to hold your ceremony in the same location as your reception, which is also quite correct, although outdoor ceremonies are not considered as formal as those held inside. You will need to hire your own officiant for ceremonies not held in a house of worship and he or she must be booked well in advance. (See chapter 8 for more information about ceremonies.)

THE RECEPTION SITE

Consider all the options when it comes to choosing the perfect place for your reception. Formality, cost, convenience, time of day, and time of year are all factors in your choice, so let your vision guide you. No site is more correct than another, as long as your guests are comfortable; it is as proper to have an oyster roast on the beach as it is to have a sit-down dinner in a grand hotel ballroom.

HOTELS   Hotels are wonderful one-stop shopping sites for wedding receptions and can usually provide everything for your reception from ice sculptures to wedding cakes in-house. The additional benefit of the hotel wedding is, of course, that all guests can stay at the hotel, which creates camaraderie among out-of-town guests and a generally festive atmosphere. Since hotels may host several weddings in a day, and hundreds in the course of a year, care should be taken to avoid a cookie-cutter effect. Keep in mind also that there may be a wedding scheduled in the same ballroom right after yours so there won't be any way to extend your reception. Modern hotels and their ballrooms may be remarkably similar from city to city, so if you're lucky enough to live in a city that boasts a wonderful historic hotel, take advantage of your good fortune.

COUNTRY CLUBS   If the bride's parents have belonged to a country club for years, and the pool is the one where she took her first swimming lessons, having a wedding reception there might feel like a homecoming. Country clubs, like hotels, are enormously experienced when it comes to weddings and can help guide you through the planning process with ease. Often country clubs are free to members and book on a first-come first-serve basis. Some country clubs require that nonmembers pay a fee and be sponsored by a club member; others are open to the public for events. Like hotels, they may hold several receptions in one day, so be sure to check and see if you'll be under the gun to wind down the party.

RESTAURANTS   If your reception is small, a favorite restaurant may be a terrific choice for your reception. Some restaurants may even let you take over the entire space to accommodate a larger guest count. Keep in mind, though, that feeding forty or fifty guests in one sitting is very different than feeding many guests at different times, so that the menu may limited to a couple of choices and overall food quality may differ somewhat from the restaurant's usual standard.

AT HOME   If the bride's parents' home, and usually garden, is large enough, there really is no place as charming for a wedding or reception or both. The charm is twofold if the house is the one the bride grew up in. It is doubtful that parents will have to undergo *Father of the Bride*-scale renovations, but do know that an at-home wedding can bring all those "I've been meaning to fix, prune, paint, plant, cut, trim, wash, pave that" projects to a head. The price of rentals should be considered, as well as the cost of additional insurance, valet parking, off-site catering, and the feelings of neighbors. During the wedding weekend, parents should have as few guests staying in the house as possible; none is an ideal number. Houseguests shuffling around in bathrobes looking for cereal can unwittingly put themselves in the line of fire when they ask innocently "Where's . . . ?" at the precise time the host realizes the rental company has dropped off 300 chairs on the front lawn instead of the back.

OTHER SITES   Many cities boast wonderful, out-of-the-ordinary wedding and reception sites. Museums, historic houses, botanical gardens, parks, and even boats can broaden the number of reception site choices. Keep in mind that many of these venues are open to the public and subsequently may only be available for evening weddings. Keeping costs in mind is essential prior to booking these sites. If you have to rent every table and chair for your ceremony and reception, things can get expensive. In addition to finding out about catering (do they have an in-house caterer or can you hire one of your choice?), liquor laws (are you able to serve liquor on the premises?), insurance (do you have to purchase insurance to hold your event there?), timing (if the building is open to the public, will the caterer, floral designer, and other vendors have access prior to closing time?), be sure to ask what sort of electrical provisions the building maintains as well. A historic house may not have the correct power configuration to accommodate the seven-piece rock band you've always dreamed of having at your reception. If you plan to have either your ceremony or reception outdoors, be optimistic, but none the less prepare for the possibility of inclement weather, and the cost of a tent.

One Wedding, One Reception, One Party

❧

My fiancé and I have just begun planning our wedding (six months away) and we've realized we really don't want to undergo all the stress that's involved in planning a huge formal wedding (not to mention the expense). What we'd like to do is have a very small wedding hosted by my parents—about twenty very close friends and family, followed by dinner at our favorite restaurant. After we get back from our honeymoon (with a two-week breather) my fiancé and I want to throw a big, informal party to include those who were invited to the wedding, plus a larger group of friends and family. (The party, therefore, will happen exactly four weeks after the wedding.) How should we handle invitations to this party? Will people be offended that they weren't invited to the wedding?

A_s long as both your families are in agreement that a small, private wedding and reception is the way to go, I see no reason to launch into planning a wedding that neither you nor your fiancé want. Agreement here is the key. If your mother has always envisioned playing hostess to 150 of her closest friends and family while 9 of your cousins attend you as bridesmaids, you're going to have problems. The groom's family should be well apprised of and in compliance with this arrangement, although technically, they don't have the final say as to the size and formality of the wedding. Because you and your fiancé will be hosting the post wedding party, the invitations should be issued in your names. Since the party *celebrates your marriage, they cannot be postmarked prior to the fact. Have your invitations mailed the day of your wedding; four weeks in advance is sufficient leeway for an invitation to an informal party. Since you'll be on your honeymoon for two weeks, including your telephone number on the RSVP line may lead to problems. If you have an answering machine, you run the risk of running out of tape or stacking up so many messages that potential guests get bored with the beep and hang up prior to leaving a message. If you have voice mail, the idea of your spending your honeymoon making a guest list to the daily refrain of "You have ten new messages in your mailbox" is too dreadful to contemplate. I recommend, therefore, that you enlist a great friend immediately and have his/her telephone number printed on the invitation. This great friend will be responsible for compiling your guest list. Promises (and delivery) of a lovely gift, purchased on your honeymoon, will go a long way to sweeten the deal.*

No, people won't be offended that they weren't invited to the (small, private) wedding under the following circumstances:

- *Guests who are not invited to the wedding should not be included in showers. No one should feel compelled to attend one leg of your wedding, so to speak, bearing gifts, without being invited to the main event.*

- *Only wedding guests are under any obligation to buy you a wedding gift. Inquiries from marriage celebration guests as to "Where are you registered?" should be met with "Really, this is a celebration. We've gotten so many gifts already, there's nothing more we need." If they buy you a gift anyway, so be it.*

The Private Wedding with a Party Later

IF taste or budget dictates, it is perfectly correct to have a small, private family wedding, followed, some time later, by a party celebrating the marriage. This works particularly well if the bride and groom are to be married in some far-off place (out of the country for instance) or at a generally inconvenient time (Christmas Eve perhaps). Public figures and those who for whatever reasons have an abnormally large circle of friends and acquaintances, may be well served by this plan as well.

Destination Weddings

IF it is your heart's desire to get married on the beach in Maui, go right ahead. Just don't expect all your relatives, who live on the East Coast, to be jumping up and down for joy. A much more thoughtful way to accomplish (almost) the same effect, is to marry where at least some of the people who love you the most can attend without undue financial hardship, then go to Maui for your honeymoon and stand on the beach all you want. If, however, you simply must have a destination wedding, invitations need to be sent very far in advance (six months is not unreasonable) in order to ensure that guests are able to secure plane tickets and lodging at the most reasonable prices. Couples should reconsider any "no children" rules, which would not be fair, nor should they schedule their weddings during the school year if they expect couples with school-age children to attend. By the way, no matter how far away the wedding, or how costly the airfare, guests may not offer their presence as a present.

Theme Weddings

IF, for instance, you are holding your reception at a botanical garden, you may certainly have a fern engraved on your invitation and perhaps give packages of flower bulbs as favors—this lends the affair a feeling of continuity. It is not, however, a theme. The "theme" of a wedding and reception is love and marriage; there is no reason to expand upon the issue. Plans, therefore, to put the bridal party into medieval costumes to complete the "knights of the round table" motif should be abandoned immediately. Costumes are for Halloween and for events that invite you to "come as your favorite TV sitcom star of the sixties and seventies" or what have you. You may use whatever colors you'd like for your flowers, tablecloths, bridesmaids' dresses, and so on. This selection does not constitute a theme either; it is merely a reflection of personal taste. No matter how big a sports fan either the bride or groom may be, colors obviously duplicating those worn by specific athletic teams don't underscore the inherent gravity of a wedding ceremony.

Degrees of Formality

ONCE you have chosen your date, time, ceremony, and reception site, you will be able to begin choosing the degree of formality for your ceremony and reception. The following is a guideline:

VERY FORMAL
A morning (usually around 11:00 A.M.) ceremony at a church or synagogue. The bride and groom usually have a large wedding party and there are usually more than 200 guests. A seated wedding breakfast (actually lunch, but always called breakfast) is held afterwards. Music

is live. Invitations are engraved. (See chapter 6 for information on invitations and wording.)

OR

An evening (starting at or after six) ceremony at a church or synagogue. The bride and groom usually have a large wedding party and there are more than 200 guests. A seated dinner is held afterwards. Music is live. Invitations are engraved.

FORMAL

The ceremony may be held at any time of day, at a church, synagogue, or other location. The bride and groom don't usually have more than six attendants each. The reception coincides with a mealtime. The meal may be seated or served buffet style. Music is live. The invitations need not be engraved.

INFORMAL

The ceremony may be held at any time of day, at a church, synagogue, or other location. The bride and groom needn't have more than one attendant each. The reception does not need to coincide with a mealtime. The food is served buffet style or is butlered. Music may be live or provided by a DJ. Invitations need not be engraved and may be extended via a personal note or even telephone call.

What's Appropriate to Wear

ONCE you have decided on how formal or informal you'd like your wedding to be, it's time to shop for clothes. Consistency is a must. A bride who has decided on an informal wedding shouldn't order a silver silk-satin dress with a five-foot train. If she does, and her groom awaits her at the altar in khakis and a blue blazer, guests will think that his tuxedo was stolen. Keep in mind too that if you're engaged to a gentleman who refuses to wear black tie, white tie, or a morning coat, you're not going to have a formal wedding.

PROPER DRESS FOR A VERY FORMAL DAYTIME WEDDING

- *The bride:* A floor-length dress, in some shade of white or silver with a long train and long veil.

- *The groom and groomsmen:* Dark gray or black morning coat, gray striped trousers, waistcoat, white shirt, black lace-up shoes, gray ascot tie.

- *The bridesmaids:* Long dresses in any color but black without sequins or any other evening wear embellishment.

- *Flower girls and ring bearers:* Children should be dressed like children not like scaled down versions of the adults in the wedding party. Little boys should not wear black tie, and little girls needn't wear a miniature version of the bridesmaids' dress. Children should dress as though they are going to church or synagogue for a special occasion—a bar mitzvah or Christmas services, for instance.

- *Mother of the bride, mother of the groom:* Street-length afternoon dresses or suits (not business suits), showstopping hats, and gloves.

- *Fathers:* The father of the bride should dress the same as the groom. If the groom's father is not participating in the ceremony or receiving line, he may dress the same as the guests.

- *Guests, ladies:* Street-length afternoon dresses or suits (again, not business suits) hats, and gloves.

- *Guests, gentlemen:* Dark suits.

PROPER DRESS FOR A VERY FORMAL EVENING WEDDING

- *The bride:* A floor-length dress, in some shade of white or silver with a long train and long veil, perhaps with evening wear embellishments, such as sequins and crystals.

- *The groom and groomsmen:* Black tailcoat and trousers, white wing-collared shirt, white piqué bow tie, and waistcoat. Black patent-leather lace-up shoes, white gloves.

- *The bridesmaids:* Long dresses in any color but black; may be embellished with sequins or crystals.

- *Flower girls and ring bearers:* Attire should be the same as it is for the very formal daytime wedding (see page 47).

- *Mother of the bride, mother of the groom:* Floor-length evening dresses in any color but black or white. Evening shoes (not leather), evening bags.

- *Fathers:* Father of the bride dresses exactly as the groom. Father of the groom not participating in the ceremony or receiving line dresses exactly the same as the guests.

- *Guests, ladies:* Floor-length evening dresses. Evening shoes (not leather), evening bags.

- *Guests, gentlemen:* Black tie, which consists of a black dinner jacket and trousers, cummerbund or waistcoat, white pleated spread-collar shirt, black bow tie, black patent-leather or plain leather lace-up shoes or tuxedo slippers.

PROPER DRESS FOR A FORMAL DAYTIME WEDDING

- *The bride:* Long dress in any shade of white or a very pale pastel, with a short or no train; veil not longer than the train.

- *The groom and groomsmen:* Club or stroller coat with striped trousers, gray four-in-hand tie, white fold-down collar shirt, black lace-up shoes.

- *The bridesmaids:* Long dresses in any color but black without sequins or any other evening wear embellishment.

- *Flower girls and ring bearers:* Attire should be the same as it is for the very formal daytime wedding (see page 47).

- *Mother of the bride, mother of the groom:* Street-length afternoon dresses or suits (not business suits), showstopping hats, and gloves.

- *Fathers:* Father of the bride, exactly the same as the groom. Father of the groom, the same as the groom, or if not participating in the ceremony or receiving line, a dark business suit.

- *Guests, ladies:* Street-length afternoon dresses or suits (again, not business suits) hats, and gloves.

- *Guests, gentlemen:* Dark suits.

PROPER DRESS FOR A FORMAL EVENING WEDDING

- *The bride:* Long dress in any shade of white or a very pale pastel, with a short or no train, veil not longer than the train, perhaps with evening wear embellishments such as sequins or crystals.

- *Groom and groomsmen:* Black tie, which consists of a black dinner jacket and trousers, cummerbund or waistcoat, white pleated spread-collar shirt (wing collars are for white tie only) black bow tie, black lace-up shoes or tuxedo slippers.

- *The bridesmaids:* Long dresses in any color but black with; may embellish with sequins or crystals.

- *Flower girls and ring bearers:* Attire should be the same as it is for the very formal daytime wedding (see page 47)

- *Mother of the bride, mother of the groom:* Floor-length evening dresses in any color but black or white. Evening shoes (not leather), evening bags.

- *Fathers:* The father of the bride, same as the groom. The father of the groom,the same as the groom, or if not participating the ceremony or receiving line, a dark business suit.

PROPER DRESS FOR AN INFORMAL WEDDING (DAYTIME OR EVENING)

- *The bride:* A street-length dress or suit in any shade of white or pale pastel color. A hat or flowers in the hair.

- *The groom and groomsmen:* Dark business suits, or less formally, navy blazers and khaki or gray flannel trousers. Festive looking ties.

- *The bridesmaids:* Street-length dresses or suits in any color but black.

- *Flower girls and ring bearers:* Attire should be the same as it is for the very formal daytime wedding (see page 47).

- *Mother of the bride, mother of the groom:* Street-length dresses or suits in any color but black or white.

- *Fathers:* Father of the bride, the same as the groom. Father of the groom, the same as the groom.

- *Guests, ladies:* Street-length dresses or suits.

- *Guests, gentlemen:* The same as the groom.

SEMI-FORMAL

If you want gentlemen to turn up in anything from black tie to blue blazers, but all the women to appear in cocktail dresses or full-length gowns (many furious at their husbands/dates for being underdressed), then spread the word that this is your dress preference.

SECOND MARRIAGES

WHAT THE BRIDE WEARS   The bride may wear any color she chooses, including white. She should not, however, even at a very formal wedding, wear a veil, nor should her dress have a train—both of which are associated with first weddings. Brides who are marrying for the second time and older brides marrying for the first time may not make use of their advanced years to justify black bridesmaids' dresses. "All my girls are in their thirties (or forties or fifties), they've worn a hundred silly dresses, it just makes more sense for them to wear black" is a statement that precedes a breach of etiquette.

WHAT THE GROOM WEARS   The degree of formality and time of his wedding, no matter how many times he's been married, dictate the groom's style of dress.

Wedding Day Reflections

I *recently went to a "black tie optional" wedding in a tuxedo. The bride's former (and my current) boss was there, and she kept commenting to me, and to some other work people, how she couldn't believe I wore a tux. It made me feel really self-conscious, and almost as if, as "just a work friend," I shouldn't have dressed up.*
—Simon

The Black Tie Dilemma

YEARS ago, it was understood that any wedding beginning at or after 6:00 P.M. mandated black tie for guests. In an effort to presumably

Moms' Outfits

❧

*My daughter is getting married outdoors this August at 3:30 P.M.
Her gown is floor-length raw silk taffeta with no train; the
bridesmaids are wearing dark pink, straight, ankle-length linen
skirts and white sleeveless linen tops; the gentlemen are wearing
white shirts, khakis, navy linen jackets and turquoise silk ties.
My question is this, what do the mother of the groom and I
wear? Since the color scheme is pink and white, should we
wear outfits to coordinate with that? My daughter tells me
that the groom's mother has her eye on a long beige, two-piece
outfit with a sequined jacket. I think we're going to look
silly wearing long skirts in the middle of the afternoon,
but I don't want to offend the groom's mother, whom
I have not yet met, by being underdressed.*

First, I would like to congratulate your daughter for having selected what sound
like absolutely charming bridesmaids' ensembles. Brides, instead of just speculating whether their maids "can wear them again" ought to ask themselves "Would I
pick this dress to wear to the next formal/informal/casual wedding I go to?" If the
answer is "No, everyone will think I'm a bridesmaid," then they've chosen a dress

relieve gentlemen who do not own tuxedos of the hassle of renting
them, this rule has regrettably been relaxed. Some brides attempt to
please everyone by putting "Black Tie Optional" on some portion of
the invitation, reply card, or other wedding-related correspondence.
(See chapter 6 for more information on invitations.) Unfortunately,

that, after the wedding, will go straight to a high-school drama department. But we were talking about your outfit, weren't we? Since neither you nor the groom's mother are members of the wedding party, you are not compelled to comply with schemes, color or otherwise. You're right, you are going to look silly wearing long skirts in the middle of the afternoon. Long skirts are for the ladies in the wedding party only, not for mothers or guests. What you have here is a formal afternoon wedding (I base this on the bride's dress, even though the bridesmaids' dresses aren't quite full-length and the gentlemen are underdressed). I suggest you wear a pale, street-length dress or suit (not a business suit), gloves, and a fabulous hat. You should choose your outfit first (as soon as possible, before the beige outfit goes on sale), then inform the groom's mother of your choice. If, after having been informed of your selection, she then chooses to go ahead in floor-length sequins, so be it. The bride, by the way, does not in any way attempt to coerce either her mother or future mother-in-law into buying coordinating "moms' outfits." The other part of your wedding day outfit will be the ubiquitous corsage. Since many ladies are now fed up with putting pinholes in perfectly good silk dresses, florists are becoming a little more creative. This does not mean wrist corsages, as though one were going to the prom. Small nosegays may be carried; flowers can be pinned to your purse, or your hat. Tempting though it may be, do not issue flowers to anyone but yourself and the groom's mother. Should grandmothers receive flowers, presumably favorite great aunts not in receipt of the same are likely to become increasingly bitter as the day progresses. Resentful elderly ladies holding a hat pin in one hand and a glass of champagne in the other are not the recipe for fun.

this doesn't work very well, or more often, at all. What this democratic attempt at a solution ends up accomplishing is a sort of class system or hierarchy among guests. The folks in black tie are sometimes regarded as overdressed or even "stuck up" by other guests. Conversely, those in black tie may speculate whether or not guests in suits are either too cheap or too insolvent to rent a tuxedo, or, even worse, that they just didn't think the event warranted the trouble. If you are going to have a formal evening wedding, it's a good idea to start spreading the word from the get go. You'll get an enormous amount of feedback; most of which will go something like this:

"There's no way your Uncle Mort will wear a tux—no way."

Response: "That's fine—just as long as he doesn't mind being dressed differently than everyone else."

"My friends won't come if they have to wear a tux."

Response: "That's such a shame, it means so much to me that they'll be there."

"If you tell people they have to wear a tux, no one will come."

Response: "Well, I hope people who really care about us will come—I guess it's going to be an intimate evening."

Just keep in mind that it's not rude to expect people to come to your wedding properly dressed. It is rude, however, to point out to any guest at your wedding, even one in shorts and a T-shirt, that they are underdressed.

Etiquette for Family and Guests

UNLESS you're asked for them, it's probably best to keep your opinions to yourself. During this stage of their engagement, the bride and groom are bombarded by suggestions, questions and comments and your not adding to the fray will no doubt be greatly appreciated. Once you get wind of a black-tie dress code, you can either buy or plan to rent a tuxedo or prepare to turn down the invitation. Gentlemen do

Dos & Don'ts

🌿

Do remain flexible when choosing a date.

Do book your ceremony site and minister well in advance.

Do realize that popular reception sites book a year or more in advance.

Do explore out-of-the-ordinary sites.

Do consider an at-home wedding.

Do make sure that your whole wedding party is dressed to the same degree of formality.

Do spread the word early on if you'd like guests to wear black tie to your reception.

Don't create a "theme" wedding.

Don't shop for a dress until you've established the degree of formality for your wedding.

Don't make moms wear coordinating outfits that don't suit them.

Don't have a veil and train if you're getting married for the second time.

not petition the groom to change the bride's mind, nor are the groom's attempts to smooth his friends' ruffled feathers by saying, "Oh, that's just for the older guys—you guys can wear what you want" to be taken seriously.

4

ALWAYS A BRIDESMAID . . .

ETIQUETTE AND ATTENDANTS

BEING SURROUNDED BY a hand-picked group of your closest friends and family can be one of the most delightful aspects of your wedding day, therefore, care should be taken when selecting your attendants. If your wedding is to be a small affair, it's perfectly all right to simply choose one attendant each, explaining to other candidates that your wedding is going to be very small but you'd love to include them as guests. In this chapter I'll explore all the aspects of choosing, dressing, thanking, and being an attendant. I'll also address some tough etiquette situations, as well as how to deal with potential conflicts between you and your attendants. Additionally, I have included etiquette advice for your friends and guests.

Choosing Attendants

IT is customary to choose attendants very soon after your engagement, usually within a couple of weeks. You should ask your attendants in

Obligation . . . or Interrogation?

❧

I have been engaged for a month and have finalized (or so I thought) my selections for my wedding party. I've chosen my only sister as maid of honor, my fiance's sister and three close friends as bridesmaids, and my niece as flower girl. A friend of mine, Susan, with who I am not especially close is good friends with one of my bridesmaids, Janet, so I do see Susan quite often socially. I was talking to Susan and Janet about the wedding party and when I said I finished choosing my bridesmaids, Susan burst into tears! She has since been petitioning Janet to get herself included in the wedding party. I feel manipulated and don't think I'm obligated to include her just because she's a "friend of a friend." Also, my mother is putting pressure on me to include my two cousins. My mother and her sister have always been extremely close and these cousins are my aunt's two daughters. I'm not close to either one of them since they are not only six and seven years younger than I am, but we did not grow up in the same city. Am I obligated to include them? Where do I draw the line—and how do I do it diplomatically?

person, if possible, or via telephone. You may have as many or as few attendants as you wish with two being the standard minimum. The bride and groom should endeavor to include their siblings in each other's wedding party (not to do so indicates a family quarrel), often siblings (or in the groom's case, his father), will occupy the roles of

These are two very different problems with two very different solutions. Susan is obviously having a gut reaction to the fact that she was counting on being included in your wedding. While her response seems rather extreme, it is not one that requires you to take action. You must, however, make it clear to her that no amount of behind-the-scenes campaigning will change your decision—her manipulation is not acceptable. Accomplishing this without another crying scene or more hurt feelings will require great tact. Resist the temptation to make your position clear by saying, "Look, the only reason we're even friends is because of Janet, okay?" Instead, approach her with something like: "I am so flattered that you want to be my bridesmaid—it's so expensive and time consuming. As you know, I've made my final decision about bridesmaids, and the choice was really hard, but I'd love it if you'd be a program or guest book attendant." If she really wants to be in the wedding, she'll accept this assignment. In any case, you must also make it clear to Janet that you no longer will accept her role as middleman.

As for the second problem, the answer is easy: You must include your cousins. The closeness between your aunt and your mother makes me think they have probably been dreaming of their daughters' roles in each others' weddings since the two women were little girls. Consider it an honor to be in the position to make their dreams come true.

maid/matron of honor or best man. This is a practical choice that alleviates the awful chore of having to choose from one's group of friends. If you do have to select an honor attendant from among your friends, simply pick whoever is closest to you. Since an honor attendant's duties involve more than just those performed on the wedding day itself, you may also wish to narrow down the candidates to those who live in your city. Since the bride's mother acts as hostess, she should not be asked to participate in the wedding party. Groomsmen may double as ushers providing you have a sufficient number of them (one per fifty guests) or you may have ushers who are not also groomsmen or a combination of both.

THE "OUT" CLAUSE

When inviting a friend or family member to be part of your wedding, you must give him or her an "out" clause. Unless the candidate answers "Yes, I'd love to!" immediately, you should certainly say "Why don't you just think about it and call me back next week?" It should not hurt your feelings to know that your old college roommate, whom you've seen only three times since graduation, is not necessarily thrilled by the thought of buying a plane ticket, a wedding gift, and a dress with matching shoes, all for the honor of being in your wedding.

MATCHING ATTENDANTS

Gone are the times when the bride's and groom's attendants were as closely matched as carriage horses. At a modern wedding it is not necessary to have an equal number of ladies and gentlemen in the wedding party. In the event of uneven wedding parties, well-intentioned endeavors to "even things up" often lead to either the bride's or the groom's asking relative strangers to be part of the wedding. Unfortunately, these token attendants often end up feeling left out, not only because they don't know you very well, but because they have nothing at all to say when the inevitable "remember the time when . . ." conversations pop up between you and "real" attendants. Stick to asking your closest friends and family, even if it means three groomsmen and five bridesmaids. (See chapter 8 for proper recessional and processional order.)

WHEN THE BRIDE HAS A BEST MAN
AND THE GROOM HAS A MAID OF HONOR

It is perfectly correct for the bride to have a best man (*not* called a "Gentleman of Honor") and/or the groom to have a maid/matron of honor (*not* called a "Best Woman"). Honor attendants dress just as the other same sex members of the wedding party do (no ladies in tuxedos please) and carry flowers in the case of a maid/matron of honor. Please see Chapter 8 for proper recessional and processional order.

LONG-LOST FRIENDS AND EX-FRIENDS

If you were an attendant in someone else's wedding years ago and have since lost close contact with them, for whatever reason, it is neither practical nor necessary to ask them to be in your wedding. When you make the call to ask someone to be in your wedding party, and find yourself repeating your first name and possibly adding your last name in order to identify yourself properly, you no longer know the person on the other line well enough to ask the question. Endeavors to make up after a falling out by asking an ex-friend to be in your wedding can be tricky too. Wedding planning is challenging enough without reliving past discrepancies and nurturing shaky relationships. However, you are welcome to try and, if things don't work out, feel free to refer to the "Firing Attendants" section of this chapter.

HONORARY ATTENDANTS

A recent and unfortunate trend is to include "honorary" attendants, who are actually attending the wedding, in a wedding program. "Honorary" attendants should be those who, due to pressing circumstances, are unable to attend the wedding as one of your wedding party or at all. Listing those in attendance as "honorary" gives the unfortunate impression that they are the folks who just didn't make the cut or who couldn't afford the dress. You may certainly include legitimate "honorary" attendants in your program, along with the reason for their absence, in the following manner:

Honorary Bridesmaid:
Mary Jane Smith
Ms. Smith is unable to attend due to her
continued commitment to the Peace Corps in Somalia.

ATTENDANTS AND PERSONAL APPEARANCE

The selection of attendants is based on inner beauty and friendship rather than physical attributes. Your wedding, while you may strive to make it beautiful, is not a beauty pageant. Excluding those persons whose weight or pregnancies make fitting into a conventional dress or tuxedo difficult is simply cruel. If an attendant's physical appearance requires that their wedding costume be specially made or tailored, then so be it. Excluding a potential attendant on the basis of a disability is unimaginable. Those whose physical limitations make a trip up the aisle prohibitively time-consuming or taxing may simply enter and leave from the altar end of the church.

Selecting the Attendant's Outfits

BEFORE selecting your attendant's outfits, be sure to review the "What to Wear" section of chapter 3, which details appropriate attire for each member of the wedding party by type of wedding.

BRIDESMAIDS

Bridesmaids wear whatever the bride has chosen for them. Period. Bridesmaids acquainted with a bride whose taste in clothes is less than fabulous should have known that all along and need not be surprised by the lemon yellow sequined chiffon number with matching hat. On the other hand, brides, instead of just speculating whether or not their maids "can wear the dress again" ought to ask themselves, instead, "Would I pick this dress to wear to the next formal/informal/ casual wedding I go to?" If the answer is "No, everyone would think I'm a bridesmaid," then they're in danger of choosing a dress that will end up being donated to a high school drama department. It is also no longer necessary for everyone's outfit to be exactly the same—a bride may select a dress in several different styles of the same fabric and let her attendants choose the one that suits them the best. The maid/matron of honor may wear a dress in a completely different color or style than the bridesmaids, or she may be dressed exactly the same. Bridesmaids should not be asked to wear the same jewelry or makeup or hairstyles. If a bridesmaid strongly objects to wearing or even refuses to wear the dress, it is unlikely the problem is simply a sartorial one. The bride should, however, find out whether or not the *price* of the dress is the source of the difficulty. If the bride's resources are sufficient, she may certainly offer to

Wedding Day Reflections

I *didn't designate an honor attendant. My two best college friends were my bridesmaids; one held my bouquet during the vows, one read during the ceremony. I told them they could wear whatever they liked—although they didn't shop together—the dresses they chose coordinated beautifully. As a result, they both looked really relaxed and lovely.*

—Diana

offset part of the cost of the dress. This is a personal favor, however, not a requirement. If the root of the problem is simply "bridesmaid behaving badly," refer to the "Firing Attendants" section of this chapter.

THE BEST MAN, GROOMSMEN, AND USHERS

Groomsmen and the best man should be dressed exactly like the groom. However, those who own their own tuxedos (black, of course) need not be forced into renting one just because everyone else is going to be in notched, rather than shawl, collars. Ushers who are

(continues on page 66)

Bridesmaids' Hairdos and Tattoos

❧

I am in my mid-twenties and have always been conservative in my appearance. I'm serving as maid of honor for my best friend (who lives in a different city); her wedding is five weeks away. I have recently changed careers and feel now that I'd like to completely change the way that I look. First, I'm going to get a tasteful tattoo on my left ankle. Second, I'm planning to change my hair color (to bright red) and style (shaved on one side, long on the other). The thing is, my appointments for both fall about a week before the wedding. (Both the tattoo artist and the hairstylist stay very booked and these were the earliest dates I could secure.) My question is, should I let the bride know or just surprise her? The dresses we've selected are short and will show the tattoo.

SURPRISE HER? SURPRISE HER? Oh, she'll be surprised all right. In fact, your turning up at the rehearsal dinner with a shock of fire engine red hair may be just enough to put her over the edge. Brides usually labor under the assumption that, after months of meticulous planning, shock and astonishment will not be part of their big day. Since this bride is your best friend, I can't imagine why you haven't already told her about your big plan, unless, of course, you are concealing it for fear of disapproval. Herein lies the difficulty. While I congratulate you on your new career and think that, in one's mid-twenties, one might sport whatever hairdo one fancies and all the tattoos one cares for, I must advise you that your timing needs improvement. By the same token I will say that brides *are supposed to select their attendants based on love and friendship, not on looks. The idea that potential bridesmaids can be weeded out because they're too tall, too fat, too pregnant, or too funny looking does not bear scrutiny. Had you always had unconventional hairdos and tattoos, I would consider it insensitive of the bride to now ask you to grow an ash blonde bob and undergo laser surgery as a prerequisite to your participating in her wedding. However, since you describe your past and present look as conservative, you must do one of the following:*

- *Abandon your plan until after the wedding. This prohibits you from even trying out the idea. No fair calling up the bride and saying things like "You know, I was thinking, just thinking, of having my head half shaved. Hah! Just joking!" Believe me, the closer the wedding date, the more selective the bride's sense of humor.*

- *Call the bride and apprise her of your plan. I tend to doubt she'll say "Terrific! I can't wait to see how it looks!" but if she does (on more than one occasion, also, you must give her at least two days to change her mind and call you back with, "You know, I've been thinking . . . ") then go right ahead. If your statement is met by stony silence followed by "You're WHAT? I can't BELIEVE THIS! Are you trying to ruin my wedding?" you must immediately back down and say "No, no. What I MEANT to say is that I'm having it all done the week after your wedding." This should diffuse the situation. By the time you're showing your hairstylist the new tattoo the bride will be on her honeymoon, no doubt reflecting on other things.*

(continued from page 63)

not also groomsmen may either be dressed the same as the grooms-men or one degree of formality down. For example, if the grooms-men were in white tie, the ushers might be in black tie. If the groomsmen are in black tie, the ushers may be in dark suits. I would also add that "creative" tuxedos should be avoided. They are the twenty-first century equivalent of the exceptionally unfortunate col-ored tuxedos and ruffled shirts of the last century. (See chapter 3 for more information on what to wear.)

Including Children in the Wedding Party

CHILDREN in the wedding party can certainly be a delightful addi-tion. Care, however, should be taken not to choose children whose age prohibits their performing predictably. Generally, children un-der four years of age ought not to be selected to act as flower girl or ring bearer. It is essential that the children, like any other member of the wedding party, attend and pay attention at the rehearsal. They and their parents should also attend the rehearsal dinner. During the ceremony parents of young attendants should be seated as close to the altar as possible, giving them the ability to instruct or remove the children if necessary. If your reception is going to last well into the evening, a babysitter should be provided to care for children in the wedding party, and take them, if necessary, back to the hotel for bed.

THE BRIDE AND/OR GROOM'S CHILDREN IN THE WEDDING PARTY

If either the bride or groom has children, it is essential that they be in-cluded in the wedding party. However, if the children are under four, they may make their way up the aisle, then simply sit in the front row. Children may certainly fill the role of honor attendants. Young boys, however, do not give their mothers away since it is a contradiction to "give away" the person on whom one depends for all of life's basic needs.

Who Pays for What?

PARENTS of the children in the wedding party are responsible for the children's clothing and the family's transportation to the wedding if they are from out of town. The bride's family should hire and pay for a babysitter if necessary. Members of the wedding party are responsible for their own wedding clothing and so great care must be taken by the bride and groom not to select outfits that are prohibitively expensive. The attendants also pay for their transportation to the wedding destination. The bride's family pays for the entire wedding party's transportation to and from the ceremony and reception. Traditionally, the bride's family is responsible for the bride's attendants lodging; and the groom is responsible for his attendants' lodging, although this is no longer a requirement.

Duties of the Wedding Party: Who Is Responsible for What

WHEN you ask a dear friend or family member to be in your wedding, it's quite an honor, but it's also quite a large task. Help your attendants know what roles they're supposed to fill so nothing gets left undone, and no one gets overworked. [NA] indicates optional.

MAID/MATRON OF HONOR

Buy her dress, turn up for fittings on time, refrain from complaining about the look/cost of dress.

Keep track of the other bridesmaids and their dresses: have they ordered? have they had their fitting? listen to them complain, etc.[**NA**]

Assist the bride, as needed, with wedding planning (thoughtful maids of honor are better served by purchasing, as a gift to the bride, several hours of a consultant's time). [**NA**]

Organize a bachelorette party or pre-wedding-all-ladies-dinner or what have you, which, as I'm sure you're aware, does not include dressing up the bride in a wedding veil that you and the other bridesmaids have thoughtfully decorated with condoms.

Attend the rehearsal and rehearsal dinner. If necessary, assist in monitoring the bride's sobriety at the latter.

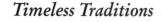

Timeless Traditions

Originally attendants dressed exactly like the bride and groom in order to confuse evil spirits. It is now a popular choice to give bridesmaids dress stipulations— any shade of pink, floor-length, with sleeves, for instance—and allow the bridesmaids to choose whichever dress fulfills the criteria.

Help organize and attend the bridesmaids' luncheon—which inevitably features silly "girl" food like curried chicken salad in a Boston lettuce leaf—when what you all really want is a cheeseburger.

Calm the bride as she waits to make her trip down the aisle. Crying jags should be avoided at this time; even so, all relevant parties should be wearing waterproof mascara.

Be responsible for the groom's ring (even if there's a ring bearer, you should have the real ring, unless, of course, the ring bearer is old enough to be responsible for the ring. Unfortunately, this often coincides with his no longer being cute).

Hold the bride's bouquet during the ceremony and adjust her train/veil before she goes back up the aisle.

Bustle the bride's dress if necessary.

Sign the marriage certificate as a witness.

Stand in the receiving line.

Dance with the best man and all groomsmen at the reception. (Bridesmaids may not spend the entire reception all at one table drinking bourbon and complaining that "I'm never going to find anyone.")

Make a toast at the reception. The best man offers the first toast, and if you are to make one also, much should be done to encourage him to accomplish his task early on. The reason I say this is because the moment you don't feel nervous any more and don't think you need to stick to your notes usually coincides with your having had too many glasses of champagne to really make sense.[NA]

Help or find someone lucid enough (bored preteens are especially suited to this task), to keep track of all the gifts that thoughtless guests bring to the reception.

Make sure the bride gets all her things together for the honeymoon. If she has a going away outfit, help her change out of her dress. Do note that wedding dresses tend to come with lots of buttons and, after a three-hour reception, maids of honor tend not to be as dexterous as the bride would like. The bride's mother (sometimes) makes a fine pinch hitter in this scenario. If much difficulty is encountered, random guests may be enlisted. Suggestions to "Just cut off the buttons" should be ignored.

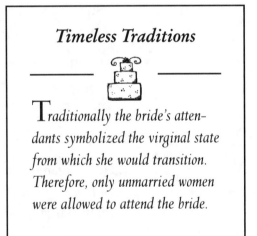

Timeless Traditions

Traditionally the bride's attendants symbolized the virginal state from which she would transition. Therefore, only unmarried women were allowed to attend the bride.

Long after one's interest in the wedding has waned, continue to answer questions—"I know you'll know this, being maid of honor. Did Hope get our gift? We brought it to the reception and we haven't heard from her. I DO hope the tag didn't fall off . . . "

Keep nagging the bride about writing thank you notes.[NA]

BEST MAN

Rent or buy your wedding clothes, show up for fittings on time, refrain from comments such as "ties should be outlawed."

Keep track of groomsmen and their fittings (have they ordered?), etc. Listen but do not encourage them to complain about wearing "monkey suits." [NA]

Organize and participate in a bachelor party. Although still considered correct, traditional debaucheries are giving way to more restrained get-togethers. The bachelor party, for obvious reasons, does not occur the evening prior to the wedding.

Attend the rehearsal and rehearsal dinner. Keep in mind that toasting at the latter does not relieve you of your duty to toast during the wedding reception.

If necessary, monitor the groom's sobriety at the rehearsal dinner.

Help organize an activity equivalent to the bridesmaids' lunch. Golf is popular, weather permitting, although any activity other than "hanging out drinking" is acceptable.

Be responsible for the groom's punctual arrival at the ceremony location.

Distribute boutonnieres to the correct persons. Relying on bridesmaids or other ladies to pin on the boutonnieres is unsound.

Usually they are off being photographed when you need them most. Ideally, all groomsmen should be able to properly tie their own ties. However, you must know how to in the event that they don't. Again, do not rely on the ladies, they have quite enough to contend with already.

Be prepared for the groom's mind to become completely unhinged prior to the ceremony. All details, including such necessities as the whereabouts of the marriage license, are likely to remove themselves, with astonishing entirety, from the groom's consciousness. You must remain calm and think for him. Many people will be asking him questions during this time. It's prudent for you to know the answers.

Be responsible for the bride's ring.

Give the fee to the officiant. Although it is the groom's responsibility to establish the amount of the fee and to provide it, it is your responsibility to deliver it. If you fear being overwhelmed on the wedding day, you may lessen your burden by giving the fee to the officiant after the rehearsal.

Escort the maid/matron of honor out of the ceremony.

Sign the marriage license.

Stand, without complaint, in the receiving line.

Dance with the bride, the maid/matron of honor, and all the bridesmaids. This is a duty and not subject to amendment.

Make a fabulous toast. No one likes speaking in front of a crowd. In fact it rates highest on people's dread list—above death. Knowing that your audience is thinking "I would sooner die than be in his shoes" rather than "I could sure do better than that, as soon as he sits down I'm going to make my own speech," should make your delivery a little easier.

Make sure the groom has everything together for the honeymoon—tickets, passports, luggage, cash for the taxi, tips, etc.

Supervise and participate, with restraint, in the decoration of the "get away" car.[**NA**]

Return, if necessary, the groom's rented clothes. Deliver and pick up any other of the groom's wedding clothes to and from the dry cleaner.

Make sure the gentlemen in the wedding party return their rented clothes on time. (Usually the Sunday after the wedding.)

ATTENDANTS

Being supportive and helpful are the number one duties of the bridesmaids and groomsmen during the engagement. Attendants do not bother the bride and groom unduly about travel plans or costs, nor do they gossip about the suitability or attitude of other attendants. Meeting all deadlines associated with fittings and alterations is essential, and once a final decision has been made, attendants cease to complain about the selection of clothing. Attendants participate in a bachelor or bachelorette party and assist in planning the same. Should an attendant find that he or she is not up to the task of being in the wedding party, for whatever reason, he or she should speak up in a noncombative fashion as early as possible. Punctuality during the wedding weekend is a must, especially for the rehearsal, when it is regrettably common to find attendants moseying in half an hour after the scheduled start time. The

Wedding Day Reflections

I had always envisioned having only my best friend as maid of honor and no bridesmaids. My fiancé and I were on a skiing holiday when he proposed, and my cousin was vacationing with us; subsequently, she was the first person I told. She hugged me and said, "Great, I can be a bridesmaid!" I was so taken aback, I ended up agreeing.

—Ruth

bridesmaids usually participate in a bridesmaids' lunch. The grooms-men more typically play golf or some other sport in lieu of lunching. If there is dancing at the reception, bridesmaids and groomsmen are required to dance with each other. Married attendants adhere to this rule also; it is absurd to imagine that married persons may dance only with their spouse. Single ladies and gentlemen in the wedding party do not petition the bride or groom to change the processional order in an endeavor to be paired with the "cutest one." Nor do they com-plain about the looks, height, or marital status of the attendant with whom they proceed up or down the aisle. (See chapter 7 for showers.)

Firing Attendants

As you move forward with your wedding planning you may be sur-prised to find that everyone does not treat you with the deference and kindness that you think should be afforded to those persons engaged to be married. Disagreements between you and your attendants often stem from financial disputes—"I'm the only one who can't afford the dress" or "Jeez, I didn't know I was gonna have to rent a tux." If you like, you may diffuse the situation by assisting with the cost, or you may simply say "I know this is going to be awfully expensive for you, so I'd much rather you come as a guest than spend too much in order to be in my wedding." The attendant in question is then free to either buck up and pay or take you up on your suggestion. Attendants who are not fulfilling their obligation to be helpful and supportive, or who are being troublesome and destructive (usually because they feel left out or not as close to you since your engagement), may be met with the following option: "I've noticed that my choosing you to be in my wedding has really caused some problems between us. I know we don't spend time together like we used to, and that's why I thought it would be fun for you to be in the wedding, but if it's causing you

Dos & Don'ts

❧

Do include your siblings in your wedding party.

Do attempt to include your closest friends in your wedding party.

Do keep in mind the cost when selecting the attendants' clothes.

Do include your children in the wedding party.

Do give your attendants a heartfelt gift of appreciation.

Do give attendants who are misbehaving the option of backing out.

Do make sure your attendants are aware of their responsibilities.

Don't make all your attendants look exactly the same, down to matching nail polish or socks.

Don't include or exclude attendants based on looks.

Don't ask children under four to be in the wedding party.

Don't dress children like mini-adults.

stress, I'll understand if you'd rather come as a guest." If the attendant in question still doesn't back out, I'm afraid, short of their doing something really awful, you must grin and bear it and hope the person returns to their old, sane self after the wedding. Remember that it's a mistake to assume that after you're married, you won't need your friends any more.

Gifts for Attendants

THE bride and groom give their respective attendants a small gift in appreciation of their friendship and support. The gifts may be anything you like. Often they are engraved to commemorate the occasion and are usually given to attendants at either the rehearsal dinner or the bridesmaids' lunch and the gentlemen's equivalent.

Etiquette for Friends and Guests Who Are Not Members of the Wedding Party

GOOD friends who are not selected to be in the wedding party keep their disappointment to themselves and wait patiently to be asked to give a reading, or attend the guest book, or hand out programs. They may also wait to be asked to usher guests. If no position of honor is bestowed upon them, they refrain from comment. Guests whose spouses are in the wedding party may not attempt to jockey for a corresponding position in order keep them company. Guests keep all negative comments about the overall looks of the wedding party, including the bridesmaids' dresses, to themselves. Friends and guests also refrain from asking attendants who have been "dating forever" whether or not "it'll be your turn next."

5

THE HONOUR OF YOUR PRESENCE

ETIQUETTE AND THE GUEST LIST

CREATING THE GUEST LIST can be tricky, especially if one family is much larger than the other or the majority of one lives in the city where the wedding will take place whereas the other one will be required to travel. If both families live in the same town and have many friends in common, dividing the guest list becomes a great deal easier. Keeping the guest list down to a reasonable number is, without question, the simplest way to stick to your budget. This endeavor, however, is probably the cause of the most wedding planning conflicts. This chapter will help you adhere to your original number with tact and diplomacy. Whether your guest list is 500 or 10, it's important to know who to invite and, perhaps more importantly, who not to invite.

Dividing the Guest List

A fair division of the guest list is as follows: parents of the bride 30%, parents of the groom 30%, bride and groom 40%. Clearly, if the bride's family is much larger than the groom's, or vice versa, allowances must be made. This is also true if one side's guests live in the city where the wedding will take place, which of course makes it more likely that they'll be able to attend. I often meet with brides and grooms who have an enormous guest list, far greater than their budget will allow; yet they cheerfully say, "Oh, no one will come." You'll be surprised just how many will come, count on roughly 70% of those invited to attend. If you feel the percentage will be much lower, you've probably invited people who should receive a wedding announcement or an invitation to the wedding ceremony only. Once you've settled on the number of guests that you'd like to attend your wedding, it's time to get down to the business of creating the list. Let parents know the total number you'd like to invite, say 200 guests, which gives them each a total of 60 guests, and you and your fiance a total of 80 guests. Parents should include family in their lists, while the bride and groom's list should include only friends. All potential guests, by the way, should receive a printed invitation. If you don't know someone's address, now is the time to find out. Verbal invitations and "bulletin-board" invitations designed to invite a group of people are disastrous; hosts of even the most informal wedding still need to know how many guests to expect.

Creating the Guest List

IT's easiest in the long run to be able to give the calligrapher, or whoever will be addressing the envelopes, the information on a disk. Handwritten lists can easily lead to misspellings; therefore, everyone should agree on a word-processing program and create their lists accordingly. Once the guest lists are in from all parties, duplications can be removed and, if necessary, the process of cutting the guest list can begin.

WHOM TO INVITE

It is extremely likely that when you let parents know the number of guests they'll be able to invite, you'll hear this sort of thing:

> "What d'you mean sixty? Just your grandparents, aunts, uncles, and cousins add up to twenty!"

> "Well I think we should be able to invite more, I mean we *are* paying for it."

> "This is ridiculous, we won't be able to ask any of your father's/mother's business friends."

Use good sense when it comes to numbers. If the groom's parents live far away and it's unlikely that they'll have enough guests travelling the distance to make up their side of the list, then the bride's family may take up the slack. If the bride and groom don't have many friends, their side of the list may diminish, freeing up the excess for both sets of parents. However the divisions take place, it is important to remember your budget and the maximum number of guests you can afford to entertain. In the strictest sense, those persons invited to your wedding should be 1) family or 2) friends (the kind that either you or your parents would invite to your respective houses for dinner). Work associates, clients, and other professional contacts who do not fall into these categories may be either invited to the ceremony only, which requires neither a RSVP nor a gift, or they may be sent wedding announcements, which also carry no obligation for either a response or presents. Very distant relatives or those who will not or cannot travel a great distance to the wedding should also be notified in this manner. To send a wedding and reception invitation to someone that you absolutely know can't or won't attend will appear as though you're scavenging for gifts. See chapter 6 for more information on invitations and announcements.

Verbal Invitations

❧

I'm getting married in six months; the wedding will be followed by a sit-down dinner. A guest list has been established and a total of 225 persons will be invited. Hopefully around 170 will attend. When we divided the total guest list between me, my fiance, and our parents we came upon a problem. Unbeknownst to my mom, my future mother-in-law has already verbally invited about 30 of her work associates in addition to her share of the 225. This throws the count. The site we've chosen for our reception can only accommodate 175 people for a sit-down dinner. When my fiance's mom found out about this, she was furious because now she'll have to uninvite all these work people so that she can invite closer friends. Could we perhaps hold two receptions? The original one, which my parents will throw and a less expensive, casual reception for work associates, etc., which my fiance and I would throw a few weeks after the wedding.

Your future mother-in-law cannot uninvite anyone because she hasn't actually invited anyone to begin with. To properly invite someone to a wedding, their name and address should be given to, in this case, your mother, who will subsequently issue a written invitation in your parents' names. Persons who receive such an invitation may consider themselves officially invited. "Y'all come" has a limited rate of success because people either tend not to take the invitation seriously, never responding one way or the other, or to consider the event to be a sort of free for all to which they happily bring along 12 of their own guests. Friends and family should be invited to both the wedding and reception, work associates *(unless they are friends and I mean true friends who engage in social activities completely unrelated to work) or their families, should not. Will she be inviting the copier repairperson? The mail carrier? By the same token, work associates who are burdened daily with the convoluted logistics of someone else's wedding planning, often preceded with "Just let me vent for five minutes," begin to feel, after a few months, that they deserve a front row seat.*

Having two receptions for two different classes of guest, so to speak, is not a good idea. Guests will only find out that the lavishness of one does not match the other and will subsequently wonder why they weren't on the "A" list. This is what I suggest: Work associates should be invited to the wedding and not the reception. This is quite standard procedure accomplished by simply sending the wedding in-vitation without the reception card. If people inquire as to why they weren't in-vited to the reception, one need only say, "Space just doesn't permit us to have as large a guest list as we'd hoped. I hope you'll be able to share the day by coming to the wedding though."

Since twenty people have already received "verbal invitations" though, I also pro-pose the following: You may trim your family's guest list in order to accommodate the extras invited by your fiancé's mother. Since the invitations have not been sent, this is still possible. You may change the format of your reception in order to en-tertain more guests. A reception site can hold up to 50% more persons for a stand-up reception than for a sit-down dinner. This early on in your wedding planning, it's a good idea to remain flexible. It is also an excellent idea to keep your future mother-in-law fully abreast of your wedding plans. Had she known the reception site could accommodate only 175, and that the total number of guests she and her husband could invite was only around 68, this problem may never have occurred.

THE BACKUP GUEST LIST

After you receive a "no" response from someone you were certain would attend you may choose to send an invitation to someone who was not on the original guest list. Take into account that this procedure is problematic because once invitations have been sent, word gets around. If this "backup" person is acquainted with other guests, and receives an invitation three weeks after they do, they may well realize that they're a second thought. If, however, the backup guest does not know other guests, he or she may just think that the bride and groom are tardy in their invitation mailing. If you do choose to create a backup guest list, you should track the "no" replies and subsequently the invitations sent to other guests very carefully to avoid miscounts. Keep in mind that it is not unheard of for a guest to call just before the wedding and say "I know we RSVP'd 'no' but Carol's business trip has been rescheduled so we'll be able to come after all!"

SIGNIFICANT OTHERS

Couples who have set up housekeeping together but are not married are considered a social unit and the wedding invitation must be extended to both parties (one invitation, addressed to both persons). Those who disapprove of such a lifestyle and invite only one of the couple in order to make a point are being rude. Couples who have not set up housekeeping but who are a recognized unit (the litmus test for this is: do you always say one name with the other?) are also invited (two invitations, one to each address.)

GUESTS' GUESTS

It is not correct to assume that all single people are uncomfortable being so and therefore cannot venture into any social situation without a date. When making up your guest list you count single guests as one person not as two in anticipation that they'll round up a date from somewhere after you write "and guest" on the inner envelope. If, by the time you mail your invitations, you find that one of your guests has a new beau, go ahead and invite them. The way to do this is to find out their name and address and mail them an invitation. You are not obligated to invite brand new girlfriends or boyfriends. In addition, guests shouldn't get huffy because you're not going to invite the charming person they met at an all-night diner the week prior to your wedding.

OFFICE CONDUCT

Contrary to popular belief, you are under no obligation to invite your co-workers to your wedding unless they are also friends outside the workplace. This being the case, proper conduct at the office during your engagement is essential if you wish to avoid hurt feelings or bruised egos. This means you neither take advantage of unlimited computer and Internet access to facilitate your wedding planning, nor do you give all your wedding vendors your work number (or even your cell phone number, if you plan to answer it at work). You do not spend the six months of your engagement chatting endlessly about centerpieces, hors d'oeuvres, and carving stations to co-workers, neither do you ask them for personal advice (you'll get plenty of that without solicitation) about wedding planning, nor do you ask them to "cover" for you when your wedding vendor meetings run long. If you do, then fail to extend invitations, your co-workers will feel snubbed at the least and you'll find that your professional standing may suffer.

> ### Wedding Day Reflections
>
>
>
> *When I got engaged I decided to invite my boss and my work's management team to the wedding. They all RSVP'd "yes," but soon after I received the responses I changed careers. Everyone from my old office still came to the wedding, but in retrospect, I probably shouldn't have invited them in the first place. Since I hadn't seen or talked to any of them since quitting my job, it felt awkward having them at the wedding. I also felt they wouldn't have RSVP'd "yes" if they'd known I was leaving.*
>
> —Sheila

Inviting Children

❧

My son is getting married this fall; the bride's niece and nephew (ages five and seven) will be serving as flower girl and ring bearer. The wedding is at 6:00 P.M. and the reception will last until about 11:00 P.M. Since there are obviously going to be children at the wedding, may we include children on our side of the guest list? I have an older, married daughter who will be traveling from out of town, and I really don't know if she'd be able to come if she couldn't bring her children aged sixteen months and three.

What you have described are children who are in the wedding as opposed to children who are guests at the wedding. Young children tend to enjoy parties that include cake and ice cream, games, and presents. They also like to be the center of attention. At a wedding that should not be the case even if the children are the bride's or groom's. Grown-up reception games like "Let's talk about who's marriage has failed and whether or not this one is going to last" are rather more subtle than the ones children really enjoy, like tag. Since you are describing a late evening reception, this is what I suggest. Do not invite small children. They'll get bored at the reception and will probably be tired and cranky just about the time mom and dad get up to join the conga line. The way to do this is to invite "Mr. and Mrs. John Smith" on the outside envelope and "Mr. and Mrs.

INCLUDING OR EXCLUDING CHILDREN

You'll need to figure out early on whether or not you wish children to be present at your wedding and reception. There is no formal policy of etiquette that dictates their exclusion or inclusion except, of

Smith" on the inside envelope, as opposed to "Mr. and Mrs. John Smith, Ted Smith, Sarah Smith" on the inside envelope. Mr. and Mrs. Smith, who may think you made an oversight, are quite likely to ring you and say, "May we bring Ted and Sarah?" to which you reply "Oh, I really don't think they'd enjoy it. I'm afraid they'd be frightfully bored, and I'd hate for you two to have to leave early to take them home/back to the hotel." You should also consider hiring a couple of babysitters for the evening. One to stay at the hotel and look after out-of-town children and one to stay at a home in town to look after native offspring. I strongly recommend that arrangement for your grandchildren. Perhaps your daughter cannot travel out of town without them, but there's no reason she could not leave them with a babysitter of your choosing in order to enjoy the evening fully. The children who are in the wedding should also be picked up and taken home or back to the hotel early. There is no reason for a five-year-old to hang around a wedding reception until eleven or so. If your son were having an afternoon wedding, things would be different. Small children (providing the reception doesn't coincide with naptime) tend to be a lot cheerier at 1:00 P.M. than at 10:00 P.M. and a lot less obtrusive at lunchtime than at a highly extended cocktail hour. Children who would rather their crudités be run though a blender prior to eating them should remain at a reception for about as long as it takes for said crudités to be digested.

course, the formality of your reception, the time of the reception, and the age of the children. Children under eight can't possibly be expected to sit still and behave through a full Catholic Mass that begins at seven in the evening. Nor can they be expected to have much decorum at a five-course, plated dinner that starts at 8:30 following a cocktail hour. Remember, with the exception of the children in your wedding party, your "children/no children" policy must be in place for *all* guests. You may not allow your sister to bring her three because they're angels and you know they'll behave without extending the same courtesy to everyone else's children. You may not print the words "No Children" on any wedding-related correspondence. You may, however, spread the word if anyone asks. You can of course offer up excuses such as: "The ceremony is going to go on for ages. It's just what we've always wanted, but it would be awful for kids." Or "The reception is at a historic house, it's absolutely filled to the brim with antiques, and there's nowhere outside to play. It would be so terrible if something got broken."

Reserving Hotel Rooms for Guests

WHEN you have a fairly good idea of how many out-of-town guests you'll be inviting, and the potential number of how many will actually attend your wedding, it's time to reserve a block of hotel rooms. Most hotels will offer a group rate for weddings, based on a minimum percentage of the block's being reserved. The hotel will give you a code for your guests to use, and, generally, they require that reservations be made by several weeks prior to the wedding. It's a good idea to give guests a couple of price ranges to choose from. For a wedding with many out-of-town guests you may reserve blocks of rooms at several hotels. You may mail or telephone this information after guests have RSVP'd affirmatively, or you may include the information on a "save the date" card.

Save the Date Cards

IF a great number of your guests will be traveling from out of town, if your wedding is to take place over a holiday weekend, or if you're simply getting married during a busy wedding month, it's extremely thoughtful to send out "save the date" cards. More formal cards match approximately the wedding invitation as far as paper color and font style. They needn't be engraved or printed in thermography. Formal wording includes the following essentials:

*Please save the date of
Saturday, the twenty-second of June
for the wedding of
Miss Julia Phillips to Mr. Christopher
Haysworth
Beaufort, South Carolina*

*Mr. and Mrs. Harold James Phillips
(if the bride's parents are hosting the wedding)
Invitation to follow*

> ### *Wedding Day Reflections*
>
>
>
> I *got a great "save the date" card from a bride who was getting married in a resort town. She'd reserved blocks of rooms at one hotel and had recommended several more. Thank goodness for the recommendations. The day I received the card I called the "blocked" hotel and they'd already sold out. I reserved at one of the other hotels, which turned out great because it was across the street, literally, from the church.*
>
> —Susan

For less formal affairs, the card may come in the form of a simple postcard, or the bride and groom may want to write a note to guests themselves. For weddings that take place over a holiday weekend, or at any time when hotel rooms are at a premium, it makes good sense to include relevant information in the card. For example:

Since Beaufort is such a lovely seaside resort, hotels and bed and
breakfasts fill up quickly during the summer.
We've reserved a block of rooms at The Bay Street Inn
(include phone number)
for a rate of $110 per night; this includes breakfast.
Please call the number above and mention the Phillips/Haysworth
wedding when you make your reservation. We also recommend
The Magnolia Inn at $115 per night (include phone number)
and The Live Oak Bed and Breakfast at $105 per night
(include phone number).

"Save the date" cards do not require an RSVP or any recognition of receipt, which you may want to make plain on the actual card. Don't include too much information, such as directions from the hotel to the church, because guests will invariably leave them stuck to their refrigerators at home. (See chapter 14 for more on information packages for hotel guests.) If your wedding is to take place on a Saturday evening and you expect that many guests will arrive on Friday, you may wish to make them aware of activities available to them on Friday evening and Saturday afternoon. You may include shopping and movie options that are close to the hotels or a list of restaurants close by or in walking distance.

DESTINATION WEDDINGS

If you are planning a destination wedding then "save the date" cards are an absolute must. They should be sent at least six months prior to the wedding, although as much as a year ahead is not unheard of. The cards must include detailed information concerning airline ticket prices and hotel recommendations and costs.

Dos & Don'ts

Do decide how many guests you'd like to have at your wedding before making up the guest list.

Do plan to send every potential guest an invitation.

Do invite both halves of a couple who have set up housekeeping together.

Do invite significant others.

Do consider hiring a babysitter for out-of-town guests.

Do reserve blocks of rooms for out-of-town guests.

Do send "save the date" cards if many of your guests will be traveling from out of town or if your wedding takes place over a holiday weekend.

Don't make single guests feel pressured to bring a date by inviting them "and guest."

Don't plan your wedding at work or invite colleagues who are not also friends.

Don't include children in your guest list if the wedding is going to be a late-night or a very formal affair.

Don't extend verbal or "bulletin-board" invitations.

Don't invite people you know can't attend. Send them an invitation to the ceremony only or a wedding announcement instead.

Etiquette for Friends and Guests

No matter how close you may be to the couple it is not correct to assume that you're going to receive a wedding invitation. Keep in mind that budget constraints may be at work when it comes to the guest list, or perhaps the couple wishes only to have family and perhaps

(continues on page 92)

Inviting Gay and Lesbian Couples

&

I'm getting married in three months, and we're finalizing our guest list. My cousin, who I practically grew up with, is gay and now lives in another city with his companion of six years. My whole family knows about this (our moms are sisters) and everyone is pretty much fine with it. The problem is that my fiance's family doesn't know, and is, as a group, pretty conservative. My fiancé (who has met and likes my cousin and his companion) has suggested we invite my cousin but not his companion, but I know that's not going to work. My fiancé has also suggested we could invite them both but not seat them together at the reception, also, that I take them aside and ask them to behave at the reception so the family won't catch on. This is an awful situation. I don't want to hurt my cousin and his companion, both of whom I love dearly, but by the same token, I don't want to shock my fiancé's family.

Well I'm shocked that you are actually considering taking grown people aside and instructing them on how to "behave" at your reception. Don't your cousin and his companion get out much? Do they not know how to behave in public? Were they raised by wolves? What exactly are you expecting them to do at your reception, dance on the tables? As for your fiance's suggestion that you invite one *but not the other, you're right that that won't work. You mention that he has met and likes both gentlemen, yet he considers omitting one from the guest list. I shudder. What would he have suggested if he didn't like them? Both your cousin and his companion should receive an invitation. Since they are a recognized couple, as opposed to roommates, the invitation should be addressed Mr. John Doe/Mr. Joe Smith written on two lines. In the course of your wedding conversations mention to your cousin by all means that your fiancé's family is conservative. There's no need to say anything else. Your cousin and his companion will know exactly what you mean. As for shocking your fiancé's family, I tend to doubt that the sight of two gentlemen seated together at a table of eight is likely to warrant a second glance from even the most staid dowager. When you make your introductions, you need not reveal to anyone the relationship between the two gentlemen, just as you need not reveal the relationship between a man and a woman unless they are married or engaged. For instance, you wouldn't say to your future mother-in-law: "This is my cousin John Doe and this is Jane Smith his live-in girlfriend who isn't yet officially divorced from her current, and third, husband." You would simply say, "This is my cousin John Doe, and this is Jane Smith." Titles like "just friends" and "just roommates" are designed to exclude highly personal information from introductions. Persons who make it their business to ferret out deeper meanings behind such titles, then profess to be shocked by their findings, serve themselves right.*

(continued from page 89)

three or four "best" friends in attendance. Know also that couples are not compelled to invite children, but if you know you are going to be invited (receipt of a shower invitation or a "save the date" card makes you a shoe-in) it's quite all right to ask about this ahead of your receiving it. If you receive a "save the date" card and plan to attend the wedding, make every effort to reserve your hotel rooms early.

6

FIT TO PRINT

Etiquette, Invitations, and Stationery

Your invitation tells the guest more than just the date and time of your wedding. Its style reflects the event's degree of formality and, perhaps, gives clues about the reception—an embossed urn for a reception that starts with a garden cocktail hour for instance. Invitations that are addressed and worded correctly facilitate your receiving proper replies from your guests, which, in turn, will assure you an accurate guest count. In this chapter I will provide every possible type of invitation wording and help steer you through the occasionally complicated world of invitation enclosures.

When to Send Invitations

Invitations should be sent six to eight weeks prior to the wedding date so plenty of time must be allowed for printing, especially engraving, and addressing.

Wedding Invitation Styles

JUST as most other things relative to your wedding, invitations will vary with your taste and style of your overall wedding. Choose the appropriate invitation, for example, you don't want a lacy, detailed, extravagantly decorated invitation for an outdoor picnic-style, casual ceremony.

VERY FORMAL

The most traditional and most formal type of invitation is either a folded large sheet or a smaller single sheet. The paper should be very heavy and either ivory or white. For the most formal invitation there should be no embellishments with the exception of a raised plate mark or the bride's family's crest or coat of arms embossed without color. The invitation should be engraved (on the first page of a folded sheet) in a roman typestyle with black ink. There should be two envelopes, both addressed by hand.

Timeless Traditions

Wedding invitations were always postmarked from the bride's mother's hometown, and her address always served as the RSVP location. Formal invitations are always hand canceled as opposed to machine canceled. Often social secretaries were employed to keep track of very large guest lists.

NOT SO FORMAL

Less formal invitations may be printed using thermography. They may also be embossed or otherwise embellished with whatever design the bride and groom select. The paper may be colored. Ink colors and fonts may vary and you may choose one or two envelopes.

TYPES OF PRINTING

Explore your printing options and pick the one that fits best with your invitation style.

ENGRAVING   The most formal and costly printing style—engraving produces a raised print on the front of the invitation and a corresponding depression on the reverse.

THERMOGRAPHY   Much less expensive than engraving, thermography also produces a raised print on the front of the invitation, but does not produce a depression on the reverse.

LITHOGRAPHY   Produces a flat print and is less expensive than thermography.

LASER   The least expensive of printing styles may be accomplished through a print shop or created by a savvy bride or groom. Paper weight may have to be sacrificed in order for the invitations to feed though a desktop printer properly.

HANDWRITTEN   Unless the bride's or groom's handwriting is exceptional, it is best to seek out the services of a professional calligrapher for handwritten invitations. Very formal invitations may have the name of the recipient handwritten on an otherwise engraved card.

WORDING

Wording is your preference, but again, choose appropriately based on formality.

VERY FORMAL   The most formal ceremony invitations are sent in the bride's parents' names and are worded (please see the "Wording for All Circumstances" section of this chapter for variations):

Mr. and Mrs. Harold James Phillips
request the honour of your presence

For a more personal touch:

Mr. and Mrs. Harold James Phillips
request the honour of the presence of
Mr. and Mrs. John Ross McMichael
(The entire name must be handwritten;
the use of initials is incorrect.)

at the marriage of their daughter
Julia Helen
to
Mr. John Christopher Haysworth
Saturday, the twenty-second of June
at seven o'clock
Saint Helena Episcopal Church
Beaufort, South Carolina

RSVP does not appear on an invitation to the ceremony only. The wording "honour of your presence" is reserved for invitations to a house of worship only. Note also that the Old English spelling "honour" is used for formal invitations. When Roman Catholic Mass is included in the ceremony, "and your participation in the offering of the Nuptial Mass" may appear beneath the groom's name. Spelling out the year is optional and so is "in the evening." For times indicating the half-hour "half after four o'clock" is correct, "four thirty" is not. Weddings take place at a quarter of or a quarter past any hour.

Less Formal

Mr. and Mrs. Harold James Phillips
invite you to share in our joy
as our daughter
Julia Helen

is united in marriage
with
John Christopher Haysworth
Saturday, the twenty-second of June
at seven o'clock
Saint Helena Episcopal Church
Beaufort, South Carolina

The Reception Invitation

THE reception invitation is a small card of exactly the same color and paper stock as the wedding invitation and is printed using the same method. It should be mailed with the wedding invitation to those invited to the reception as well. It reads:

Reception
immediately following the ceremony
Pine Lakes Country Club
Beaufort

The favour of a reply is requested

OR

RSVP

Note: The spellings "R.S.V.P." or R.s.v.p." also are correct. Also note that the Old English spelling "favour" is used for formal weddings.

Unless the reply should go to an address different than the one on the outer envelope of the wedding invitation, there need not be an address after the RSVP section of the reception card. It is not correct to include the words "black tie" or "white tie" on the wedding invitation. However, you may include this in the reception invitation in the lower right-hand corner.

RESPONSES

Reception invitations being sent to guests who know where the oyster fork goes in a formal place setting need no reply card. These guests know they should RSVP on their own stationery, in their own hand, with the following wording:

Mr. and Mrs. John McMichael
accept with pleasure
the kind invitation of
Mr. and Mrs. Phillips
for
Saturday, the twenty-second of June

OR

Mr. and Mrs. John McMichael
regret that they are unable to accept
the very kind invitation of
Mr. and Mrs. Phillips
for
Saturday, the twenty-second of June

OR

Mrs. John McMichael
accepts with pleasure
the kind invitation of
Mr. and Mrs. Phillips

for
Saturday, the twenty-second of June
but regrets that
Mr. McMichael
will be unable to attend

PRINTED REPLY CARDS

The likelihood of guests' handwriting replies is slim, ergot the invention of the reply card. The card is similar in size to the reception invitation and also is sent with the wedding invitation. It should be printed or engraved in the same color ink as the invitation, using the same font. It should never include the line "number attending" regardless of what you've written on the inner envelope of the invitation, because many guests will infer that this means they may bring a guest or even guests. It is also not unheard of for guests to return reply cards with nothing filled out. Therefore, it's a really good idea to pencil a number on the back of each reply card in order that blank cards may be matched with the corresponding guest and a telephone call can be made. Guests please note that is perfectly correct to disregard this card and handwrite the response on personal stationery. A reply card may be blank with only "The favour of your reply is requested" etc. printed across the top. The only problem with this is that many guests have no idea what they're supposed to write on the blank part (the exact wording they would use to reply on their own stationery). In light of this, it's best to keep confusion to a minimum and send this:

The favor (or more formally, favour) *of your reply is requested by June 14*

M_____

accepts _____

regrets _____

If the invitation has been addressed "and guest," the guest's name should be written on the reply card along with the primary invitees. If the invitation is extended to a guest or guests with children, all names should be written on the reply card also.

REPLY CARD ENVELOPES　These may be pre-addressed or left blank, in which case the guests should send them to the address on the back of the wedding invitation envelope. Whoever is responsible for giving the final guest count to vendors should receive reply cards.

Wedding Day Reflections

I had a sit-down dinner for my wedding reception, and I really didn't think about how problematic my having addressed at least fifty invitations "and guest" would be. We decided on place cards for dinner, but almost no one had included the name of their guest on the response card. We ended having to write "guest of so and so" on a lot of place cards, which seemed really impersonal.

—Anna

Enclosures

As you start looking through invitations, it may seem a little complicated, once you see all the additional enclosures you have to choose from. Here is what you're looking at—it will help you decide which one you need.

TISSUES

The printer includes tissues in a wedding invitation to prevent the ink from smudging. Although it is still correct to leave the tissues intact, modern printing methods render the practice obsolete and therefore unnecessary.

PEW CARDS

Pew cards are generally given to close friends and family. The inclusion of such cards ensures that important guests are seated close to the altar, regardless of their arrival time at the ceremony. Cards should be printed or engraved with the guest's name if they are sent with the invitation and the pew number is generally handwritten. If the bride would rather wait until responses have been received, she may send handwritten pew cards to those who RSVP "yes":

Pew Number 6
Mr. and Mrs. John McMichael

The guests should present the card to the usher who will escort them to their seats.

WITHIN THE RIBBON CARDS

If the couple doesn't wish to wait for responses in order to estimate the exact number of pews to be reserved, "within the ribbon" cards may be included with the invitation. Reserved pews are ribboned off, and ushers who escort guests who produce such a card remove the ribbon, then replace it after the guests are seated. The cards may or may not include the guests' names, they may simply read:

Within the Ribbon

ADMISSION CARDS

Unless the couple has achieved a celebrity status, or the church is a huge tourist attraction, admission cards create more problems than they solve. Invariably guests forget them, leaving ushers with the unenviable job of bouncer. If you must have them, they should be printed in the same manner as the invitations and read:

Please present this card
at
Saint Helena Episcopal Church
Saturday, the twenty-first of June

ENTRÉE CHOICE CARDS

If there is to be a choice of entrée, the service staff should ask guests for their selections at the reception. Not only is it not proper to include entrée choice cards in a wedding invitation, but by the time guests show up for the reception, they either can't remember what they've ordered anyway, or they change their minds because the salmon looks better than the filet mignon. (See chapter 9 for more information on reception food.)

MAPS AND DIRECTIONS

You may include directions from the ceremony to the reception on a separate card. However, out-of-town guests benefit from receiving directions from the hotel to the ceremony also. It is best to provide them with this information at the hotels themselves. (See chapter 13 for more information about out-of-town guests.)

GIFT REGISTRY INFORMATION

Under no circumstances, whatsoever, should gift registry information appear in a wedding invitation.

Addressing the Envelopes

FORMAL invitations should come in two envelopes. An outer, mailing envelope, on which the guests' full names appear, along with postage, and a return address on the back or front top left of the envelope.

TO A MARRIED COUPLE

Outer envelope:

Mr. and Mrs. Conrad J. King
(for the most formal invitation, the middle name must be
spelled out, for less formal, the initial may be used)

15 Wheeler Drive
Charlotte, North Carolina 28222
(the state is spelled out, not abbreviated)

The inner envelope simply bears the recipient(s') last name(s):

Mr. and Mrs. King

Although you may certainly write in family nicknames instead:

Nana and Granddaddy

You may also use just the first names of very close friends:

Jack and Maddie

TO A MARRIED COUPLE WHEN THE WIFE'S LAST NAME IS DIFFERENT:

Outer envelope (alphabetically):

Ms. Sarah L. Achenbach
Mr. Conrad King

Inner envelope:

Ms. Achenbach and Mr. King

TO AN UNMARRIED COUPLE LIVING AT THE SAME ADDRESS:

Outer envelope (alphabetically):

Mr. James D. Fosselman
Mr. Conrad L. King

Inner envelope:

Mr. Fosselman and Mr. King

Roommates living at the same address should receive their own invitations.

If you wish to invite someone to bring his or her own guest, the outer envelope should be addressed in the standard manner and the inner envelope should read:

Ms. Spence and Guest

If you invite a couple with children under sixteen, the outer envelope should read:

Mr. and Mrs. John R. McMichael

The inner envelope should read:

Mr. and Mrs. McMichael
Margaret and Ellen

If only one envelope is used, the children's names should appear on it. Do not simply write "Mr. and Mrs. McMichael and Family," which may lead them to believe that they can bring the aunt, uncle, and cousins who live next door. Children over sixteen who live at home should be sent their own invitations addressed in the same manner as an adult's.

TITLES

The following are correct uses of common titles for inner and outer envelopes:

Attorney
Outer envelope: Mr. John Ross McMichael, Esq.
Inner envelope: Mr. McMichael

Minister or Rabbi
Outer envelope: The Reverend Paul Ross Walker (or Rabbi Isaac
 Jason Burger)
Inner envelope: The Reverend McMichael (or Rabbi Burger)

Physician/Dentist/Veterinarian
Outer envelope: Dr. John Ross McMichael or John Ross
 McMichael, D.V.M
Inner envelope: Dr. McMichael

Judge
Outer envelope: The Honorable John Ross McMichael
Inner envelope: Judge McMichael

Professor
Outer envelope: Dr. John Ross McMichael, or John Ross
 McMichael, Ph.D.
Inner envelope: Dr. McMichael

The word "junior" is properly spelled out, not abbreviated and not capitalized:

Mr. John Ross, junior

The numerals "II" or "III" appear with or without a comma, both ways are correct:

Mr. John Ross, II
Mr. John Ross III

Assembling the Envelopes

THE invitation goes in the inner envelope with the text facing the flap. If the invitation is folded, it goes in the envelope spine side toward the bottom of the envelope. For a single sheet invitation, all inserts should go in front of the invitation. For folded invitations, they belong on the inside of the invitation itself. The inner envelope is never sealed. It should not, in fact, even be gummed, and it goes in the outer envelope with the front facing the outer envelope's flap. You should have your invitation, complete with all inserts, weighed properly at the post office. There is no stamp more correct than any other although "Love" is traditional. Generally, reply cards do not require extra postage, but if you are going to stamp the envelopes for these be sure to have them weighed separately.

Invitation Wording for All Circumstances

IT's important to have the appropriate wording on your invitations so you don't offend anyone or produce inaccurate information. And as you'll see, there are many different ways to word it correctly.

INVITATIONS TO BOTH
THE WEDDING AND RECEPTION
When the wedding and reception are both held at the place of worship:

Mr. and Mrs. Harold James Phillips
request the honour of your presence
at the marriage of their daughter
Julia Helen
to
Mr. John Christopher Haysworth

Saturday, the twenty-second of June
at seven o'clock
Saint Helena Episcopal Church
Beaufort, South Carolina
and afterwards at the reception

RSVP

When neither the wedding nor the reception is held at a place of worship:

Mr. and Mrs. Harold James Phillips
request the pleasure of your company
at the marriage of their daughter
Julia Helen
to
Mr. John Christopher Haysworth
Saturday, the twenty-second of June
at seven o'clock
Pine Lakes Country Club
Beaufort, South Carolina
and afterwards at the reception

RSVP

When the wedding takes place at a house of worship, but the reception is held elsewhere:

Mr. and Mrs. Harold James Phillips
request the honour of your presence
at the marriage of their daughter
Julia Helen

to
Mr. John Christopher Haysworth
Saturday, the twenty-second of June
at seven o'clock
Saint Helena Episcopal Church
and at a reception
following the ceremony
Pine Lakes Country Club
Beaufort, South Carolina

RSVP

When the wedding and reception take place at a residence:

Mr. and Mrs. Harold James Phillips
request the honour of your presence
at the marriage of their daughter
Julia Helen
to
Mr. John Christopher Haysworth
Saturday, the twenty-second of June
at seven o'clock
at the residence of Mr. and Mrs. Peter Vasseur
6233 Bay Street (may be omitted if you've enclosed a map card)
Beaufort, South Carolina
and afterwards at the reception

RSVP

INVITATIONS TO THE RECEPTION ONLY

Mr. and Mrs. Harold James Phillips
request the pleasure of your company
at the wedding reception for their daughter
Julia Helen
and
Mr. John Christopher Haysworth
Saturday, the twenty-second of June
at seven o'clock
Pine Lakes Country Club
Beaufort, South Carolina

RSVP

When the reception is not held on the same day as the wedding:

Mr. and Mrs. Harold James Phillips
request the pleasure of your company
at a reception
in honor of
Mr. and Mrs. John Haysworth
Saturday, the sixth of July
at seven o'clock
Pine Lakes Country Club
Beaufort, South Carolina

RSVP

DECEASED PARENTS

When the bride's mother is deceased:

> *Mr. Harold James Phillips*
> *requests the honour of your presence*
> *at the marriage of his daughter . . .*

When the bride's father is deceased:

> *Mrs. Harold James Phillips*
> *requests the honour of your presence*
> *at the marriage of her daughter . . .*

When both of the bride's parents are deceased, the bride and groom may issue the invitations in their names with or without the inclusion of the deceased:

> *Julia Helen Phillips*
> *daughter of the late Mr. and Mrs. Harold James Phillips*
> *and*
> *Mr. John Christopher Haysworth*
> *request the honour of your presence*
> *at their marriage . . .*

If the bride's parents are both deceased and a relative or godparent is hosting the wedding, the title "Miss" is used. If the bride was not orphaned at a young age, the wording remains the same but the title "Miss" is omitted:

> *Mr. and Mrs. Spencer Lee Phillips*
> *request the honour of your presence*
> *at the marriage of his sister*

Miss Julia Helen Phillips
daughter of the late Mr. and Mrs. Harold James Phillips
to
Mr. John Christopher Haysworth
son of Mr. and Mrs. Charles Edward Haysworth . . .

DIVORCED AND REMARRIED PARENTS

When the bride's divorced mother is hosting the wedding:

Mrs. Susan Ann Phillips
requests the honour of your presence
at the marriage of her daughter
Julia Helen
to
Mr. John Christopher Haysworth . . .

When the bride's parents are divorced and both are hosting the wedding:

Mrs. (or Ms.) Susan Ann Phillips
and
Mr. Harold James Phillips
request the honour of your presence
at the marriage of their daughter
Julia Helen
To
Mr. John Christopher Haysworth . . .

When the bride's mother has remarried and she and her husband are hosting the wedding:

Mr. and Mrs. James Patrick Howard
request the honour of your presence
at the marriage of her daughter
Julia Helen Phillips
to
Mr. John Christopher Haysworth . . .

When the bride's mother has remarried and she, her husband, and her ex-husband are hosting the wedding:

Mr. and Mrs. James Patrick Howard
and
Mr. Harold James Phillips
(or Mr. and Mrs. Harold James Phillips if he has remarried also)
request the honour of your presence
at the marriage of their daughter
Julia Helen Phillips
to
Mr. John Christopher Haysworth . . .

When the bride's parents are divorced and her father and step-mother host the wedding:

Mr. and Mrs. Harold James Phillips
request the honour of your presence
at the marriage of his daughter
Julia Helen
to
Mr. John Christopher Haysworth . . .

BRIDE AND GROOM ISSUING
THEIR OWN INVITATIONS

When the bride and groom issue their own invitations the title "Miss" is used:

The honour of your presence
is requested
at the marriage of
Miss Julia Helen Phillips
to
Mr. John Christopher Haysworth . . .

OR

Miss Julia Helen Phillips
and Mr. John Christopher Haysworth
request the honour of your presence
at their marriage . . .

OR (less formally)

Julia Phillips and John Haysworth
request the pleasure of your company
at their marriage . . .

SECOND MARRIAGES

If the bride is a young widow, her parents may issue the invitations using her married name:

Mr. and Mrs. Harold James Phillips
request the honour of your presence
at the marriage of their daughter

Julia Helen Adams

to

Mr. John Christopher Haysworth . . .

When the bride is divorced and her parents host the second wedding, she would use her married name:

Mr. and Mrs. Harold James Phillips
request the honour of your presence
at the marriage of their daughter
Julia Helen Adams
to
Mr. John Christopher Haysworth . . .

When the bride is an older divorcee she and the groom generally issue the invitations. If the bride has dropped her ex-husband's name, she uses her first name, middle name, and maiden name. If not she may use the title "Mrs." if she likes, and use her first name, maiden name, and ex-husband's name:

Julia Helen Phillips

OR

(Mrs.) Julia Phillips Adams
and Mr. John Christopher Haysworth
request the honour of your presence
at their marriage . . .

WHEN THE GROOM'S FAMILY HOSTS THE WEDDING

If the bride's family is from abroad or if some other reason prevents them from hosting the wedding, the groom's family may issue the invitations. Note the use of the title "Miss":

Mr. and Mrs. Charles Edward Haysworth
request the honour of your presence
at the marriage of
Miss Julia Helen Phillips
to
their son
John Christopher Haysworth . . .

FAMILIES CO-HOSTING

When the bride's and groom's families co-host the wedding:

Mr. and Mrs. Harold James Phillips
and
Mr. and Mrs. Charles Edward Haysworth
request the honour of your presence
at the marriage of
Julia Helen Phillips
and
John Christopher Haysworth . . .

INVITATIONS TO A DOUBLE WEDDING

At double weddings the two being married are usually sisters or they might also be cousins who have grown up extremely close to one another or exceptionally close friends.

When the brides are sisters, the oldest sister's name appears first:

Mr. and Mrs. Harold James Phillips
request the honour of your presence
at the marriage of their daughters
Julia Helen
to
Mr. John Christopher Haysworth

and

Isabel Lucinda

to

Mr. Henry Stewart Graham . . .

When the brides are cousins or unrelated, either the oldest bride's parent's names appear first, or they may be listed alphabetically:

Mr. and Mrs. Harold James Phillips

and

Mr. and Mrs. Thomas Ralph Lloyd

request the honour of your presence

at the marriage of their daughters

Julia Helen Phillips

to

Mr. John Christopher Haysworth

and

Georgina Kay Lloyd

to

Mr. Ashton James Spencer . . .

MILITARY TITLES

If the groom or bride is a member of the reserves, they may only use their military title if they are on active duty:

Captain John Haysworth

United States Marine Corps Reserve

Officers in the army whose rank is captain or higher have the title printed on the same line as their name:

Lieutenant Colonel John Haysworth

United States Army

Naval officers with the rank of lieutenant, senior grade or higher, also have their title printed on the same line as their name:

Commander John Haysworth
United States Navy

Persons with lower ranks should have their names printed in this fashion:

John Haysworth
Lieutenant, United States Army

Enlisted men and noncommissioned officers may have their rank and branch of service printed below their name:

John Haysworth
Private, United States Marine Corps

If the groom is retired from the armed forces, his title is printed in the following manner:

Vice Admiral John Haysworth
United States Navy, retired

If the bride's father is a member of the armed forces, he uses his title:

Lieutenant General and Mrs. Harold James Phillips
request the honour of your presence

If the bride's mother is a member of the armed forces she may include her title if she wishes or she may stick with "Mrs.":

Major General Mr. Harold Phillips and Susan Phillips
request the honour of your presence

When the bride is in the military her name appears on one line and her rank and branch of the military on the next:

at the marriage of their daughter
Julia Helen
Captain, United States Navy
to

PROFESSIONAL TITLES

Gentlemen may use their professional titles (this includes judges, senators, doctors, dentists, and so on) on their own wedding invitations and on those they issue. Holders of academic doctoral degrees don't usually use the title "Doctor," however.

Doctor and Mrs. Harold James Phillips
request the honour of your presence
at the marriage of their daughter
Julia Helen
to
The Reverend John Christopher Haysworth . . .

Ladies use their titles when they issue their own invitations along with the groom:

The Honorable Julia Helen Phillips
and Mr. John Christopher Haysworth
request the honour of your presence
at their marriage . . .

Wedding Announcements

IF you have many acquaintances or family who live far away and you would like to let them know, as a courtesy, that your wedding has taken place, it is correct to send wedding announcements. Announcements should be mailed the day after the wedding and should match the wedding invitations' paper, font, and degree of formality. (See chapter 5 for more information about who receives announcements.) The standard wording is as follows:

Mr. and Mrs. Harold James Phillips
have the honor of announcing
the marriage of their daughter
Julia Helen Phillips
to
Mr. John Christopher Haysworth
Saturday, the twenty-second of June
two thousand (the year is always included)
Beaufort, South Carolina

You may add the name of the church if you'd like. Announcements may certainly be handwritten, particularly if the engagement period was short or even nonexistent and there was no time for a visit to the stationer.

At-Home Cards

AT-HOME cards give the bride and groom's new address and are properly sent with a wedding announcement or invitation. They may also be placed in some conspicuous way at the reception. They read:

(continues on page 122)

Children Issuing Invitations

❧

My daughter, who has one son age three and is pregnant with another, is planning to marry her long-time boyfriend (it's about time). The child she is carrying will be one month old at the time of the wedding. My daughter wishes to include the children as much as possible and wants the invitations to be from them. How should she word these invitations? I'd do it differently, but she and her fiance are paying for everything.

The impending birth of a child is cause for great celebration and a terrific reason for a wedding. If I were you, I'd avoid statements like "it's about time," "finally," or "at last." The timeliness of this wedding is quite evident and needs no embellishment. It is wonderful that your daughter wishes to include her children in the wedding and much should be done to ensure their participation. Including them in wedding planning, however, is not practical. A three-year-old does not host his parent's wedding. Hosting his fourth birthday party will fill his plate amply. Persons unborn are in a similar predicament (though not as unfortunate) as those deceased. No matter how well loved is the departed or how precious is the expected, individuals cannot issue invitations, even as co-hosts, from either the grave or the uterus. If, however, your daughter and her fiancé had grown children from previous marriages, the invitations may be worded thus:

Mr. William Smith
Miss Janet Doe
request the honour of your presence
at the marriage of their parents
Elizabeth Susan Smith
and
Phillip John Doe . . .

In your daughter's case, however, this does not apply. If she and her fiancé are hosting the wedding, the invitations may read:

> The honour of your presence
> is requested
> at the marriage of
> Miss Elizabeth Smith
> to
> Mr. Phillip Doe . . .

OR *(less formally)*

> Elizabeth Susan Smith
> and
> Phillip John Doe
> invite you to attend
> their marriage . . .

A possible departure and really the only way to include your grandson would be:

> Elizabeth Susan Smith
> and
> Phillip John Doe
> along with their son
> William James
> invite you to attend
> their marriage . . .

I am not particularly fond of the latter wording for two reasons. It puts a three-year-old in the impossible situation of being a co-host and also draws unnecessary attention to the fact that, while they are not married, the couple in question have none the less moved forward with those activities technically granted by a marriage license.

By the way, who is paying for what makes no difference at all. The bride and groom's forking out for a reception does not give them the right to issue improper or downright odd wedding invitations. By the same token, the refrain "I'd do things differently," which I'm certain applies to more than just invitation wording in this case, should be used sparingly and never in front of grandchildren.

(continued from page 119)

At Home (or Will Be At Home)
after July fifth
593 East Main Street
Richmond, Virginia
(804) 442-7316

If you wish to include your names and the bride is changing hers, you must wait until at least the reception to distribute them:

Mr. and Mrs. John Haysworth
At home . . .

If the bride is not changing her name, you may send them prior to the wedding:

Julia Phillips and John Haysworth
At home . . .

Place Cards, Table Numbers, Menus, and Wedding Programs

It's a good idea to shop for these items at the same time as you shop for your invitations. The menu cards should be printed using the same font as the invitation; the paper ought to be the same color as well. The place cards and table numbers should be handwritten in a similar manner to your wedding invitation envelopes. It's also a good idea to order your wedding programs along with your invitations. Again, they should be coordinated with your invitation style. A wedding program should contain your order of service and include any readings, solos, or hymns. You may include the names of persons in your wedding party; you may not, however, substitute a wedding program for a receiving line or proper introduction—it should not end up looking like a playbill. In addition, wedding vendors should not be included or thanked in the program. If the altar flowers are placed in someone's memory, it is correct to include the dedication in the program.

Personal Stationery

It's also a good idea to order personal stationery along with invitations so you'll be well prepared for writing thankyou notes. Prior to the wedding brides must use their maiden name monogram; if their name is to change after the wedding, stationery must reflect this. Brides who keep their maiden names may use the same stationery before and after the wedding. Some recipients of this stationary may think it's an oversight. If they happen to ask, the bride may take the opportunity to set the record straight: "Oh no, I didn't forget to change the stationery. It's the same because so is my name." Once guests receive more than two post-wedding correspondences bearing the bride's maiden name they should get the hint and stop addressing theirs to "Mrs. John Haysworth." This includes all friends and guests, including those who don't approve of the bride keeping her name.

Wedding Day Reflections

I *got married in Las Vegas with just my best friend and my mom as guests. The chapel videotaped the ceremony and broadcasted it over the Internet. About three weeks prior to my wedding I sent my friends "invitations" to watch the wedding, which included the time, the date, and the Web site address.*

—Kathryn

Recalling the Wedding Invitations

If the wedding is canceled after the wedding invitations have been sent, a card should be sent with the following wording. (Note that even if the invitation was engraved speed is of the essence and the card should be simply printed.) If time does not permit the sending of cards, telephone calls are in order.

Mr. and Mrs. Harold James Phillips
announce that the marriage of their daughter
Julia Helen
to
Mr. John Haysworth
will not take place

If the wedding has been cancelled owing to the death of a family member, the following wording may be used. Again, if time is short, telephone calls may be made in lieu of the card.

Mr. and Mrs. Harold James Phillips
regret (or regret exceedingly)
that owing to the recent death of the brother of Mr. Haysworth
the invitations to the marriage of their daughter
Julia Helen
to
Mr. John Haysworth
must be recalled

If the wedding is postponed, a card should be sent. Reception cards should reflect the new date, and reply cards reflect a new RSVP date, if applicable:

Mr. and Mrs. Harold James Phillips
announce that the marriage of their daughter
Julia Helen
to

Mr. John Christopher Haysworth
has been postponed from
Saturday, the twenty-second of June
until Saturday, the twenty-seventh of July
at seven o'clock
Saint Helena Episcopal Church
Beaufort, South Carolina

Etiquette for Friends and Guests

FRIENDS and guests reply to wedding invitations promptly (on the day after the invitation is received if the invitation is from someone close to you and, certainly by the requested RSVP date, if one is included. If no RSVP date is offered, you should RSVP by at least two weeks prior to the wedding date). Don't call the bride and groom and ask if you may bring a guest when such an option is not indicated on the inner envelope. Do not RSVP in a manner not dictated by the invitation (which includes "write-in" guests and special requests such as "vegetarian dinner required"). If no reply card is enclosed, you should reply by hand in the manner mentioned in this chapter. Don't call the bride and say "Hey, I got your invitation but you forgot to put in one of those little cards." Don't consider yourself to have RSVP'd because you saw the bride in the mall and said, "Can't wait for the wedding!" Do not RSVP via telephone or e-mail unless the invitation gives you the tools to do so. If your plans change after you RSVP (and by that I don't mean you get another invitation to a wedding you'd prefer to attend), you write, or call if time is short, the person(s) who issued the invitation. Your excuse for not coming, by the way, had better be good. Under no circumstances do you attempt to ascertain whether or not the wedding is worth your attending by quizzing the bride about the style of her reception.

Dos & Don'ts

❧

Do give yourself plenty of time to order invitations, especially if they're engraved.

Do mail your invitations six to eight weeks prior to your wedding.

Do number the back of your reply cards in case respondents forget to fill in their names.

Do send wedding announcements if your guest list was small or to those who you feel certain are unable to attend.

Do attempt to order all your wedding-related stationery at one time.

Do order stationery printed with your married name for post-wedding thank yous and other correspondence.

Don't put "RSVP" on an invitation to the ceremony only.

Don't include an option for "number of persons attending" on your reply card.

Don't send admission cards unless you're famous or you feel the church will be overrun with tourists.

Don't send gift-registry information with invitations.

7

THE CENTER OF ATTENTION

Etiquette for Showers and Gifts

At no other time after your engagement will you feel more at the center of attention than at the shower that your friends (hopefully) are kind enough to throw for you. Registering for wedding gifts is also lots of fun, especially since you're no longer limited to just china, silver, and crystal. There are proper procedures when it comes to gift giving and receiving, and unfortunately those who give are quick to criticize those who receive when it comes to some real or imagined lapse of graciousness. Careful attention to the guidelines in this chapter will help steer you clear of even a hint of reproach.

How and When to Register for Gifts

You may register for wedding gifts as soon as you've announced your engagement and set your wedding date; however, if your engagement lasts over six months, stores may no longer carry all the items on your registry by your wedding date. Conversely, you must, as a courtesy to your guests, be registered by the time your "save the date" cards or invitations go out. Practically every store open for business offers a wedding registry these days, with the possible exception of grocery stores, although I'm sure we won't have to wait long for that romantic option. Registering is easy, albeit time-consuming. In some stores you find what you'd like, then simply write it down on a piece of paper, then turn it in to the registry consultant. Many stores, however, give you a scanner and you just scan the bar code of whatever items you'd like, which takes a lot less time than the pen-and-paper method and can be more fun since it's easier to be impulsive with a scanner. If you are going to register for china, silver, and crystal, however, take plenty of time to look around before selecting the store or stores with which you'd like to register. The choices can be overwhelming, and grooms tend not to be as entertained by this segment of registering as they are by others. Grooms who get out of going to register by saying "What do I care about china?" relinquish all rights to judge the merits of any wedding gift bought with the aid of said registry. Most stores will also enable you to track your registry online, which is a lot more fun than ringing them up every week to see if you've got a full set of champagne glasses yet. You may eschew visiting stores all together in some cases and register online, which is easy and fast. The additional benefit of online registry is that you no longer need worry whether your guests have physical access to your favorite store. Couples may also create their own wedding page on wedding web sites, which give guests access to their entire, multi-store gift registry. Be sure to find out how long the store will continue to keep your registry open. It's a great resource for potential gift-givers during the first year or two of your marriage.

Timeless Traditions

A bride in the 1950s, in addition to a complete set of standard china, might have also registered for other tableware, including ashtrays, cigarette containers, saltcellars, oyster plates, and fish plates.

What to Register For

CHINA, silver, crystal, and linen are the most traditional wedding gifts, however, no rule of etiquette requires that you register for any of them. Probably the most important rule of registering is that the couple selects gifts within a wide price range. If you know that most of your guests' means are modest, there's not much point in registering for gifts priced well into triple digits. Since the array of stores offering wedding registries has broadened, so has the gift selection. It's easy to register for anything from toasters to office furniture to food processors to draperies. The best gifts, of course, are the ones that the couple can both enjoy.

No Gifts Please

YOU may *not* print on any part of your invitation, "save the date" card, or any other wedding correspondence "No Gifts Please." To ask guests not to send gifts is to suppose that they will in the first place—which is presumptuous. The way to discourage gift giving is to not register. When guests call to find out where the couple is registered, it's perfectly all right to say "Oh, they aren't registered. Really, I think they have everything they want." If guests then want to wander around the mall trying to find the "something for someone who has everything" gift, there's nothing to be done to stop them.

Wedding Day Reflections

When I got engaged I didn't want to do the whole registry thing. I really wanted guests to just come to our wedding and not feel under obligation to give presents. The wife of a work friend heard about this and was horrified; she absolutely insisted that I register. My husband and I finally registered, reluctantly, at a chain store. The funny thing was that the wife didn't buy us a gift from the registry, but something (not exactly useful) that she'd picked out on her own.

—Kim

Money or Donations in Lieu of Gifts

You may not ask for money as a wedding gift, even if you need it badly, although nothing prevents guests from giving it. Those who know you and your situation well will think it more practical to write checks than buy sterling flatware. You may not ask that guests give donations, no matter how worthy the cause, in lieu of gifts. If you receive money as a gift, nothing prevents you from giving it to your favorite charity. There are no exceptions to these rules.

Where the Gifts Should Be Sent

Traditionally, gifts were sent to the bride's parents' house because, until her marriage, it was also the bride's house, and all gifts, even if the giver had never even met the bride, were addressed to her. Nowadays, the gifts should be sent to the bride, although they may be addressed to her fiancé as well. Take care when you register to have the proper address on record and, if you plan to move during your engagement, have the record updated and put in a forwarding order at your old address. Gifts do not, under any circumstances, belong at the reception. This is one of the very few unbreakable rules of wedding etiquette. It's also the simplest to adhere to.

Once the Gifts Have Been Received

Gifts are fun—but getting them is not the only thing involved. Once you receive your gifts, you have some responsibilities that follow.

THANK YOU NOTES

First I would like to squelch a funny little myth that has been brought to my attention by more than one bride. Couples *do not* have a year from the receipt of a gift to write the thank you note. Guests, however, do have a year from the wedding date to give gifts. Thank you notes were once the sole responsibility of the bride; this probably stems from the assumption that she would quit her job and apply herself only to wedding planning from the moment she became engaged. There is no such rule in effect today. The groom can certainly write them all or the couple can split the task. The point is that someone has to write them, and be quick about it. The thank you should go out on the same day that the present is received. This is not a Herculean task; however, for those who are not up to it, the next day will do. The note is hand-written (*not* on cards with the words "Thank You" pre-printed any-where on them) and follows this wording approximately:

> Dear Aunt K,
>
> Thank you so much for the fantastic food processor; I've always wanted one, now I'll feel like a professional chef. John thanks you in advance for the potatoes au gratin that are sure to follow. We're so looking forward to seeing you at the wedding—only two weeks away now—time flies!
>
> Love,
> Julia

RETURNING WEDDING GIFTS

There is no rule against returning wedding gifts, in fact, if registries between stores are not updated properly, it is not unheard of to re-ceive four gravy boats and six meat platters. Naturally, if each person who gave the gravy boat comes to your house for dinner, you must tell him or her that the vessel on the table is in fact, their gift. There is obviously no point in bringing attention to this sort of duplicity, so write thank yous for all the gifts then exchange those that are super-fluous. If, on the other hand, a guest buys you something outside the gift registry that is not to your liking, even greater tact must be

The Gift Table

❧

I attended a wedding recently and was, I think, treated extremely rudely. As soon as I found out where the bride and groom were registered I bought them an entire place setting of their good china, which was quite expensive. When I entered the reception with this beautifully wrapped (and rather heavy) gift, I asked a woman (whom I later found out is an aunt of the groom) where the gift table was located. She turned to me and said, "There isn't one." When I asked where I should put the present, she rudely snapped "You should have thought of that before you brought it," and walked off. I ended up putting the gift back in my car, then dropping it at the bride's mother's house the next morning. This was all very inconvenient—am I right to assume that there should have been a secure place provided for gifts?

No, you aren't. *The bringing of gifts to receptions is nowadays so frequent an occurrence that guests have begun to think it is the correct thing to do. Hosts, presumably fed up with piling gifts on the floor, have begun to provide "gift tables," which are not to be confused with the quite correct display of opened gifts on the dining room table at the bride's parents' home. Although the aunt (and I hope you*

employed. If someone you don't expect to see at your home in the next five years has given the gift, you can certainly ascertain where he or she bought the gift, then endeavor to return it. You must, however, write the thank you for the original gift. If, on the other hand, *discovered her title in some other way than sulking around the reception randomly questioning "Who is that (insert expletive here) in the mauve sequins?") was indeed quite rude, you should have realized, in the absence of a table, that your gift, although I'm sure most appreciated, was not welcome at the reception. The correct way to be sure the wedding gift makes it securely to its rightful recipients is thus: send it. If you like, it may be sent directly to the bride's address or, if you know her address will be changing after the wedding and you are not yet privy to the new address, you may send the gift to the bride's mother's house. If you live in the same town as the bride's mother, you could certainly call ahead, then drop the present by in person. However, be sure to do this well ahead of the wedding weekend itself, when the household is likely to be in an uproar. Wedding gifts, quite unlike other gifts, are not meant to be opened in person, which is why the giver is always thanked in writing. One of the problems associated with "gift tables" is the tendency for gifts and their cards to part company with great alacrity. Once this has occurred, it's anyone's guess as to who gave what and invariably leads to people either not being thanked at all or being thanked for the "cool lava lamp" rather than "the exquisite eighteenth century English bone china." Your taking the gift to the bride's mother's house the day after the wedding was quite all right; I hope you are thanked eloquently for the sentiment behind your offering, which, as you know, has nothing to do with it being "quite expensive."*

the gift was given by someone closer, I'm afraid you'll just have to live with it (or put it away and only bring it out when the giver comes over). By the way "re-gifting" a present you don't like but can't return isn't advisable unless you're absolutely sure of two things: 1) The recipient would just adore it and 2) the original giver does not know the recipient. "Re-gifting" a really heinous present is risky because it may well complete a circuit and end up with the original giver. Presents of this caliber may be cheerfully sold at yard sales for one dollar.

GIFTS AND THE CANCELED WEDDING

In the unfortunate situation that the engagement is broken and the wedding is canceled, ALL gifts must be returned with a note. Since technically the gifts are given to the bride, it is she who returns them. (See "The Broken Engagement" in chapter 1 for note wording.)

The Shower

THE wedding shower is an old custom originating in the Netherlands. Tradition has it that a girl married a poor miller whom her parents considered unworthy. To show their dissatisfaction with the match they gave her no dowry. Overcome by the couple's predicament the townspeople rallied together and, to make up for the parents' snub, "showered" the couple with gifts. (See the "Here Comes the Bribe" section of chapter 2 for more information along these lines.)

WHO THROWS A SHOWER?

Traditionally a friend or friends of the bride give the shower. Since a shower is a fundraiser of sorts, a member of the bride's family should never give one. Friends of the groom are also welcome to host a shower. No one, however, including the maid of honor, is obligated to throw the bride a wedding shower. The shower is a charming custom taken up by those who have the means to accomplish it. It is not a right of the engaged.

THEMES

The bride and groom may drop hints or, when asked, offer suggestions for a theme, but they do not insist on one or voice their disappointment if the hostess chooses something else. Lingerie showers are traditional, as are kitchen and bath showers. Garden and bar showers are also popular, although the possibilities are endless and all equally correct.

WHEN TO THROW A SHOWER

Shower throwing can get underway as soon the engagement has been announced. Keep in mind that it's not a good idea to throw a shower the week of the wedding, even though everyone you want to invite will be in town for the event. Just like any party, there is no time of day more or less correct to hold a wedding shower. Remember, though, at parties that coincide with mealtimes, guests expect to be fed.

INVITATIONS

Generally shower invitations reflect the theme of the shower and can be just as cute or clever as the hostess wants. Since the acceptance of the invitation carries with it the

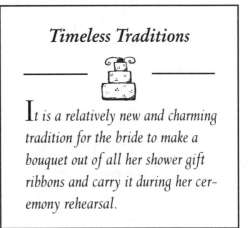

Timeless Traditions

I*t is a relatively new and charming tradition for the bride to make a bouquet out of all her shower gift ribbons and carry it during her ceremony rehearsal.*

obligation of a gift, it's polite to go to the trouble of actually sending a written one rather than telephoning or e-mailing. Response, however, may be given by phone or e-mail, as the hostess chooses. Invitation wording may approximate the following:

Laura McMichael and Susan Spence
Invite You to
a Kitchen and Bath Shower
for Julia Phillips

on
Saturday, January 20th
at
Three o'clock
6233 Hanover Avenue
Richmond
RSVP 358-9749 or susie@earthlink.net

THE GUEST LIST

If the bride is being thrown multiple showers, care must be taken not to include the same guests over and over. This is especially true of the wedding party, who, unlike other guests, may feel obligated to attend every shower. The guest list should include close friends of the bride, her sisters, mother, future mother-in-law, and close women relatives. One steadfast rule is that those who are invited to the shower must be invited to the wedding.

COED SHOWERS

It is much more modern to have coed showers than single sex, since maxims such as "The guys would be bored at a kitchen shower, they can't cook" are no longer true. The guest list should include the groom's friends and family, and a theme that interests both sexes should be chosen. Just because the party is coed, there's no need to pressure single guests into bringing a date by inviting them "and guest."

OFFICE SHOWERS

If the bride has close friends with whom she also happens to work, it's perfectly all right for them to throw her a shower on their own time. It is not all right, however, for work associates to pass the hat around the office in order to throw an "office shower." Inevitably those who do not know the bride well, or perhaps don't even care for her, end up shelling out resentfully for a gift because they don't want to look cheap or as if they don't like the bride. Doubtless everyone has plenty to contend with between the hours of nine to five without throwing parties for relative strangers. If the bride gets wind of such a scheme she should seek out the instigator and say something such as: "That's so sweet of you to think of me, but really you, Kate, and Jill are the only ones I really know in this department. How about we get together after work some night next week instead?" The bride should insist on thwarting these sorts of plans, unless of course she's perfectly happy to be obligated to invite all of the office shower attendees to her wedding. Keep in mind, however, that it is not unreasonable for co-workers who have spent months listening to every detail of courtship to feel they are entitled to a little celebration when the engagement is announced, even if they throw it themselves.

GIFTS

Gifts for a shower should not be expensive; under $30 is reasonable. Couples do not register for shower gifts, and guests should not shop the couples' wedding registry for shower presents (so that all the inexpensive gifts are gone and wedding guests who didn't go to showers are left with all the pricey choices). The hostess or host should be prepared to answer guests' gift questions, "Oh, their kitchen is navy and white," and give suggestions, "I think he'd really like a pizza stone." The bride and groom can give the hostess a "wish list" beforehand, keeping in mind the under $30 suggestion. Wish lists, by the way, don't appear on the invitation or in any other kind of written correspondence. Keep in mind that guests usually like to buy a whole gift, so it's not fair to ask for something costing $120 and expect four people to thrown in for it. Gifts should be actual, not in the form of gift certificates or money, nor should they be related in any way to wedding expenses. The "Let's Chip in for the Limo" shower is not allowed.

When Guests Won't RSVP

❧

I have rather a dilemma. My neighbor and I are hosting a shower on April 9th for another neighbor, a young lady I've known for quite some time, who as a teenager babysat my children. Anyway, the RSVP deadline on the invitations was April 1st. The bride called me a couple of weeks ago and said there were five people from work she wanted to invite and she'd get the names for me. She did not, so I figured she'd decided against inviting them. Anyway, she rang me yesterday (April 2nd) with these five names. The problem is that I only have two invitations left, and, of course, these guests will know they're an afterthought by the date of the RSVP. I really don't want to go all the way back to the stationers and have five more invitations printed with a different RSVP date. May I tell her to just invite them verbally? What about people who RSVP "yes" after the 1st? (I've already had two messages). May I tell them I've already given the count to the caterer and we can't accommodate them, or should I accept RSVPs up until the day of the event? Nine guests (including the bride's mother) haven't RSVP'd at all. What should I do about that? I am so frustrated—honestly, this is the last time I'll offer to throw a shower.

Welcome to the sometimes gruesome world of invitations and responses. To answer your first question, yes, you may ask the bride to verbally invite her work friends. Even if you did return to the stationers and have more invitations printed, guests who receive an invitation on the 4th for an event on the 9th, even with an

"RSVP by April 7th," will know that they are an afterthought. This, of course, would reflect poorly on you and your neighbor as co-hosts, even though the bride is to blame. Making her issue verbal invitations will put the burden of explanation squarely on her shoulders, which is where it should be. Brides, please pay attention. When someone is kind enough to throw a shower in your honor, you have a couple of responsibilities. One is to be gracious and grateful. The other is to provide your hosts with an accurate guest list in a timely manner. One may not, as an afterthought, add to the guest list at the last minute. It's rude. In addition, exceeding the original guest count increases the cost of catering, possibly extending your hosts' budget beyond the affordable. Now for the RSVPs. Guests, pay attention. The reason for an RSVP date on your invitation is not because the hosts needed one more line to balance out the look. It is because they are working with a deadline. Usually, they are attempting to ascertain the number of guests in order to ascertain the quantity of food and drink; caterers typically require a guest count the Monday prior to a weekend event. Hosts may be preparing the food themselves and ordering rental tables and china, which of course requires an accurate count. Regardless, it is rude to RSVP one way or the other after the specified date. Should you find yourself in that position, the tardy RSVP must come with much explanation and a sincere apology. Those who feel they need not RSVP at all are committing a high crime. Unless you wish to convey that the invitation means nothing to you, that you do not care for either the bride or her kind hosts, and that you are certainly not interested in either attending or even being invited to the impending wedding, you should RSVP as instructed. The bride's mother, by the way, who has not bothered to RSVP, will receive her just rewards, when, after painstakingly issuing 200 wedding invitations, the very same thing happens to her.

Going Broke Over Wedding Showers

          🎋

One of my closest and dearest friends asked me to be her brides-maid. I accepted gladly. That was four months ago; the wedding is in three months. Since I signed up for this, I've spent $680. The dress ("bridesmaidy") was $200, matching shoes $80, shower at my apartment $150, plus a total of $250 in gifts for four other showers. There are two more showers to go, and still, I haven't bought a wedding gift. I know I'm going to get invited to these last two showers. How can I get out of going? As far as the wedding gift goes, I want to give her something really personal, not just a place setting, but I feel something personal is going to cost more, and, frankly, I'm just about going broke over this wedding. I'm single, only one year out of college, and I don't have the money for this, period.

Going broke over a wedding is a venerable tradition, usually reserved for the bride's family. This custom has nothing to recommend it, so I advise against your attempting to throw your hat into the ring by continuing to spend $62.50 every time someone decides to "shower" the bride with gifts. As for the $680 you've already shelled out for the honor of being bridesmaid, the money's gone and you'll

SHOWERS AND SECOND WEDDINGS

Wedding showers are associated with a bride's first wedding. Even if the bride's first husband took her to the cleaners, it's not fair to ask friends and family to participate in a second shower in order to make up the shortfall. That they come across with a second wedding gift is enough to ask. Couples who are waiting for either party's final *never see it again. Don't dwell on it or ever let the recipient of your generosity get even the slightest whiff of your exasperation. Let's, instead, focus on the two remaining showers plus the wedding gift. The key here is to pace yourself so that, theoretically, you'll have more in your pocket at the reception than cab fare home. Your close and dear friend is likely to catch on if you go making up an excuse not to go to these last two showers. Unless you have a really credible justification not to (faking your own death/illness will cost you as much as a shower gift), you really should attend. I do, however, urge you to be more conservative in your gift giving. This (take heed all those involved in attending or planning weddings), need not be confused with the unfortunate concept of being "cheap." Twenty dollars is plenty of money to spend on a wedding shower gift, but, if you have your eye on a present costing three times as much, pool your resources with two other people. I imagine that you will find others on the shower guest list with a budget similar to yours. You may certainly give your friend something "really personal" as a wedding gift, just as long as it's something both she and the groom will be able to enjoy. I can't imagine, though, why a gift full of sentiment would necessarily cost more than one bought to satisfy a request.*

In closing, I'm happy to reveal that etiquette, in its mercy, has given you a full year from the wedding date to produce a special gift.

divorce papers are not technically engaged and may not be thrown wedding showers.

THANK YOU NOTES FOR SHOWER GIFTS

Unlike wedding gifts, the shower gift is opened in front of the giver and gratitude is displayed on the spot. Technically, this relieves the recipient from having to write a thank you note. Nevertheless, thoughtful couples take this opportunity to use up all the maiden-name monogrammed stationary and write sincere thank yous anyway. A thank you should also go to the host/hostess of the party.

Etiquette for Friends and Guests

GUESTS who receive and decline a wedding invitation are under no obligation to buy a gift. Guests who accept an invitation have one year from the wedding date to purchase a gift, although they may do so just as soon as they find out where the couple is registered. Guests may not, under any circumstances, bring gifts to the wedding reception. Ever. For any reason. Guests who do not receive timely thank yous for their generosity may not ask, "How come I didn't get a thank you?" They may, however, with a degree of alarm, say, "This is so awful. I just got off the phone with (insert store name) and they said that they shipped your gift three months ago and I can't believe you haven't received it." The bride/groom will then answer, "Oh no, we got it ages ago, before the wedding even." The guest may then say, "Really, well when I didn't hear from you I just figured you didn't get it, *I'm so relieved.*" If you don't receive your thank you in ten days, you're never going to get one, and I'm afraid there isn't a thing you can do about it.

Although it's always an honor to be invited to a party, showers carry with them the obligation of a gift and it's quite all right, as with

> ### *Timeless Traditions*
>
>
>
> Wedding gifts were once displayed at the bride's parents' home for guests to peruse prior to the wedding; guests could also view them at the reception held at the house. Checks were displayed with a sheet of paper covering the amount and a piece of heavy glass over that to prevent peeking. This is rarely done these days, although perfectly correct.

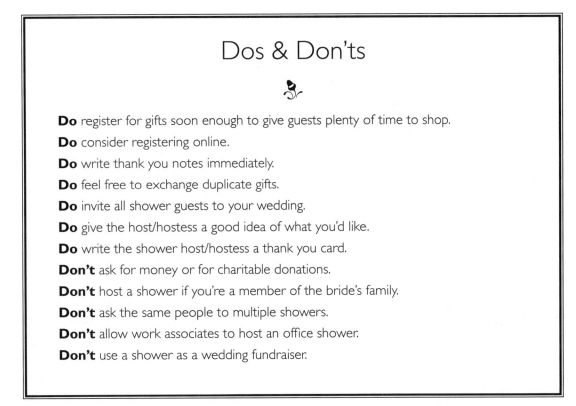

Dos & Don'ts

Do register for gifts soon enough to give guests plenty of time to shop.

Do consider registering online.

Do write thank you notes immediately.

Do feel free to exchange duplicate gifts.

Do invite all shower guests to your wedding.

Do give the host/hostess a good idea of what you'd like.

Do write the shower host/hostess a thank you card.

Don't ask for money or for charitable donations.

Don't host a shower if you're a member of the bride's family.

Don't ask the same people to multiple showers.

Don't allow work associates to host an office shower.

Don't use a shower as a wedding fundraiser.

any invitation, to decline. This is doubly justified when you've been invited to multiple showers.

Work associates please resist the well-intentioned urge to throw wedding showers at the office. If you are a good friend of the bride or groom you will doubtless be invited to a legitimate shower (one that occurs outside a workplace). If you are not close to either of them, but wish to show how happy you are for them, a really nice letter sent to their residence will suffice.

WITH THIS RING . . .

ETIQUETTE AND PLANNING THE CEREMONY

ONCE YOU AND your fiancé have decided where you will be getting married, you should arrange a meeting with your priest, rabbi, or minister. In some states notary publics are able to perform marriage ceremonies, as are private citizens who apply for a special license. In other states, only those who are ordained by a church may perform the ceremony, thus you should ascertain early on the nature of the laws of the state in which you are to be married. A great deal of protocol surrounds marriage ceremonies; this chapter will help you to ask the right questions concerning your marriage ceremony: "Can a Catholic priest marry us at our reception site, a botanical garden?" "Do I have to have someone give me away?" "Where do my divorced parents sit?" All these questions should be asked early on in order to help you avoid surprises close to your wedding day. Note that in this chapter the words "groomsman" and "usher" are used interchangeably as are "honor attendant" and "maid/matron of honor" and "best man." (See chapter 4 for more information on attendants.)

Can My "Bridesmaid" Give Me Away?

ॐ

I am an only child; my father died ten years ago. I'm going to have a private wedding with just my fiance, my mom, my best friend, and me in attendance. My best friend is a guy. My question is, is it OK for him to escort me up the aisle and give me away? He would then stand on my side of the minister as my "bridesmaid." Should my mom stand on the groom's side and is it all right for her to give the groom my ring when it's time? I know this is untraditional. Will it look weird?

Weird to whom, since there is no congregation? Since your father is deceased, your best friend really can't "give you away," unless this best friend also helped your mother to raise you, which, since you've called him "a guy," I doubt. He may, however, escort you up the aisle. The minister can either skip the "Who gives/presents?" part, or he may include it and your mother would respond "I do." Since there are no other guests, your mother will be both the first and last person to be seated. If she feels odd about being the only person to sit down, she may stand at the altar either on your side, or if symmetry is the goal, on the groom's. It is perfectly fine for her to give the groom your ring, your attendant, of course, will give you the groom's. Your attendant should also hold your bouquet and, if necessary, adjust your train. The notion that gentlemen either can't perform these duties or will "look silly" performing them is sexist. Since your wedding is so small, it is logical that your (not "bridesmaid") honor attendant, or more accurately, best man, be dressed exactly the same as the groom. Unlike a lady in his position, he does not carry flowers; a boutonniere will do nicely. Even if your mom chooses to remain seated during the ceremony (in which case, the groom should already have your ring), your best man should escort her out. By the way, the only "untraditional" part of your arrangement is that the groom has no best man. You do, however, have two witnesses to your union, the bare minimum, but correct none the less.

The Officiant

IF you belong to a church or synagogue and plan to be married there, contact the officiant as soon after the engagement as possible. You should confirm the date and time of the ceremony as well as establish the number of guests the church or synagogue can comfortably hold. You should also inform the officiant if yours is an interfaith marriage or if one of you is planning to convert to the other's religion. If you plan the ceremony for somewhere other than a church or synagogue, you need to find out whether your officiant is able to marry you. For instance, Catholic priests are only able to marry couples in a Catholic church.

If you don't belong to a church or synagogue, or if your officiant is unable to marry you because you are not getting married in a church or synagogue, or if the church does not recognize a divorce, you will have to choose an "off site" and often nondenominational officiant. Research your state laws to find out who can legally perform your marriage ceremony. Be straightforward when you meet with an officiant, particularly if one or both of you is agnostic or atheist (and a civil ceremony might work best for you), or if either of you have strong views about any part of your religion's marriage ceremony wording. If you are planning an interfaith ceremony, be sure that your officiants are willing to perform the ceremony together.

When you meet with your officiant, find out what his or her fee will be and if others involved in your wedding also require a fee (the organist, cantor, or sexton, for instance). If you have hired a wedding planner, find out whether he or she may direct your ceremony (some churches and synagogues will only allow you to use their own directors). Above all, you should feel comfortable with your officiant and share religious or spiritual views. Many religions require or recommend that couples go through premarital counseling prior to marriage. You and your fiancé should agree on whether this is right for you. The officiant and his/her spouse should be invited to the rehearsal dinner and the wedding reception. If your officiant will be present at either, establish whether he or she will offer a blessing prior to the meal.

ESSENTIAL QUESTIONS TO ASK EARLY ON

◆ Are any special certificates required of you, your fiancé, or those participating in the ceremony, such as birth certificates, baptismal certificates, or confirmation certificates?

◆ Does having attendants who are different religions create a problem? For instance, in a Catholic ceremony only the Catholic attendants may receive mass.

◆ How many weddings is the church/synagogue booked for on your date? Most churches book several weddings on any given day and it is important that you know how much time is between your wedding and the ones before and/or after yours, particularly if you plan to have a receiving line immediately after the ceremony or photography prior.

◆ When can the florist arrive? What are restrictions on flowers? Many churches/synagogues will allow you to share the cost of flowers with the wedding before and/or after yours. This can be a money saver, so be sure to find out. Many churches require you to leave your altar arrangements for the following day's services. Be certain to find this out ahead of time since, if this is the case, you won't be able to remove your flowers for use at the reception. Also, find out what restrictions there are on flowers. Many sites require that they be certain dimensions and in specific containers. Also ask if you may use petals on the aisle and if you are allowed to use an aisle runner. Ask what sort of pew markers the site has, or, if you choose to rent your own, what type do they allow (free standing or clamp on). Can your guests toss rose petals or birdseed when you leave the church? Very often you will be allowed to do this only if someone cleans up immediately afterwards. For Jewish ceremonies, ask who is to provide the chuppah or chuppah poles, for Christian ceremonies, ask who provides the unity candles.

♦ Are there any dress code restrictions? Some sites require that you and your attendants' shoulders be covered.

♦ Is photography and videography allowed? (Most churches/synagogues do not allow flash photography during the ceremony.) Where can the photographer/videographer set up during the ceremony?

♦ What time can the photographer/videographer arrive?

♦ Is there a place to dress on-site? How large is the room? Is there a room for the groom and best man to wait in?

♦ What time will you be able to rehearse? If the church is booked for several weddings on your day, rehearsal slots will be at a premium. Will the organist/musicians be present at the rehearsal?

♦ Can you have additional musicians, vocalists, or a soloist? Must they be booked through the church/synagogue? If not, when should they contact the organist and/or music director? What sort of music is allowed, only religious or secular, too?

♦ May the reader(s) read only religious text or secular also? Is there a microphone for the reader(s)?

♦ Will communion be part of the ceremony? For whom? The bride and groom only? The wedding party also? Or practicing members of the congregation as well?

The Marriage License

No one gets married without this legal contract, and the laws that define it vary from state to state. Some states require a waiting period before a marriage license can be issued; in other states the marriage license is only valid for a certain number of days. Some states require documentation such as an original social security card, all states have age restrictions, and all states require proof of divorce from those who have been previously married. Other states require that your marriage license be issued in the county in which you are to be married; still others allow you to obtain a license from any county in the state. Your officiant will be able to steer you in the right direction. If you are planning a civil ceremony, call the registrar of deeds for information.

> ## *Wedding Day Reflections*
>
>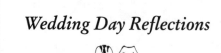
>
> **M**y *parents have been divorced for many years and a friend of my mother's is really the father figure in my life. My father and his wife were present at the wedding and I didn't want to create conflict by having my "adopted" father escort me. Eventually I decided that my dog, Bear, would be the one to accompany me up the aisle; he also acted as my only "bridesmaid."*
>
> —Christina

Vows

MANY couples choose to either write their own vows entirely (common for civil ceremonies) or amend existing religious wedding ceremonies with their own words. Again, your officiant will steer you in the proper direction. If you do choose to write your own vows, keep the following in mind:

♦ *Generally, the shorter the better.* Your friends and family do not need to be subjected to twenty-minute monologues describing your entire relationship from the first date on.

- *Don't include everything.* Sly references to sex, former boyfriends, girlfriends, wives, or husbands are in poor taste. However, if either of you have children, it is perfectly correct to include them in your vows.

- *Be positive.* "For richer, for poorer, in sickness and in heath" or words to that effect really cover everything. If you want to bring up things such as "when we argue" or "and we know there will be disagreements, even bitter at times" do so during premarriage counseling, not during the ceremony. References to how long you've dated ("I know you probably never thought we'd see this day") or to break-ups ("The two months we spent apart were the hardest of my life") do not add to the optimism essential to a wedding ceremony.

- *Have a cheat sheet.* Endeavor to memorize your vows, but be sure they're also typed on index cards (the honor attendants can keep them until the proper moment) just in case.

Transportation

As soon as you confirm your ceremony times and the number of people who will need hired cars, plan your transportation. The bride and groom and wedding party usually arrive at the ceremony and reception in limousines or other forms of transportation, and the bride and groom's parents may wish to as well. For a large wedding with many out-of-town guests, or for receptions that are held many miles from the ceremony site, you may wish to hire passenger vans or buses to transport guests. It is essential that you book your transportation—especially limousines—as early as possible. Prom season coincides with many popular wedding weekends and limousine companies are exceptionally busy and book well in advance. See chapter 14 for more information on transportation.

The Ceremony

THE following applies to religious ceremonies held at either a place of worship or at another site (a ballroom or garden, for instance). (See chapter 14 for information on ceremony programs.)

THE PROCESSIONAL

In Christian ceremonies, the last two people to be seated are the groom's mother and then, finally, the bride's. Contrary to popular belief, their being seated last is not an "honor," which requires special music and a mention in the program. The bride's mother is seated last because she is the hostess, and, as such, does not sit before all her guests are seated. Members of the bride's close family should be seated whenever they arrive at the ceremony site. Grandparents should not be required to stand around and wait until all the other guests are seated before they can take their places. The mothers may be escorted by any one of the groomsmen or ushers, however, it is unwise to assign this responsibility to the best man, who generally has too many behind-the-scenes duties to act as an escort immediately prior to the ceremony's beginning. When the bride's mother is seated, the ceremony begins and no guests should be seated after her.

Some couples prefer that the groomsmen do not proceed up the aisle, but rather assemble at the altar along with the groom and best man. If groomsmen do not assemble at the altar, they may precede the bridesmaids in single file or in pairs, or they may escort the bridesmaids and "pair off" at the altar. The flower girl and or ring bearer follow the bridesmaids, the maid/matron of honor follow them. All variations are correct, but be sure to check with your minister to confirm that the processional order you've chosen is acceptable. See figures 2–4 for examples of three standard processional lines—of course, yours will vary depending on your preference and the amount of people in your wedding party.

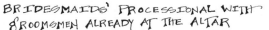

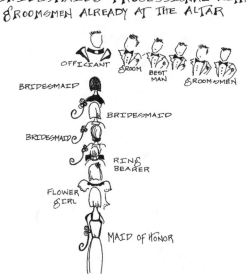

Figure 2. Standard Christian processional line (one example).

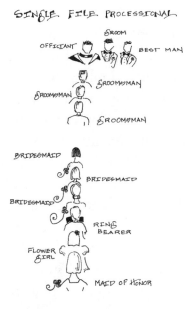

Figure 3. Standard Christian processional line (one example).

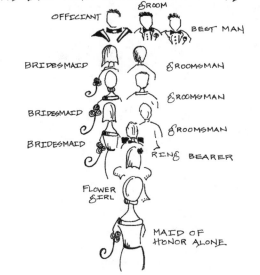

PROCESSIONAL WITH BRIDESMAIDS ESCORTED BY GROOMSMEN

Figure 4. Standard Christian processional line (one example).

In Christian ceremonies, the bride's father escorts her up the aisle. The bride walks in on her father's left arm. Generally she remains with her father at the altar until the words: "Who gives (or who presents) this woman to this man?" The father says "I do," or more commonly, "Her mother and I do," then he steps back and is seated with the bride's mother (in Catholic ceremonies, this is omitted). This procedure has been subject to much amendment in the past few years and many brides choose to eschew this tradition all together and walk the aisle alone. If the bride's father is deceased, the bride's closest male relative may escort her, or her mother can certainly take his place. The bride may also choose to be escorted by both her parents, which is perfectly correct. In this case, the groom's mother would be last to be seated.

In Jewish ceremonies, the processional begins with the rabbi and/or cantor. The grandparents of the groom are next, followed by the grandparents of the bride, the groomsmen in pairs, the best man,

Figure 5. Standard Jewish processional line.

the groom (escorted by his parents, father on his left, mother on his right), then the bridesmaids, the maid/matron of honor, the ring bearer and/or flower girl, and finally the bride escorted by her parents, father on her left, mother on her right. See figure 5 for an example of a Jewish processional.

ORDER OF SERVICE (CHRISTIAN CEREMONY)

Guests are ushered to their seats.

The parents of the groom (or only the mother of the groom if the groom's father is in the wedding party) are ushered to their seats. If the groom's mother is to light the unity side candle, she does so now.

The mother of the bride is ushered to her seat. If she is to light the unity side candle, she does so now.

If an aisle runner is to be used, it is rolled out by ushers/groomsmen.

The officiant enters the sanctuary, followed by the groom and the best man.

The bridesmaids'/groomsmen's processional music begins.

Attendants enter (see "The Processional" section of this chapter for order).

The bride's processional music begins, and she proceeds up the aisle.

In most Protestant ceremonies the order of service is as follows although readings and solos or hymns may of course be added:

Opening remarks/presentation of the bride.

Charge to the couple.

Vows.

Exchange of rings and lighting of the unity candle (very often the soloist performs during the lighting).

Pronouncement of marriage.

Kiss (it is an important rule of etiquette that the groom is always the first to kiss the bride after the ceremony).

Closing remarks/blessing/presentation of the couple ("I present Mr. and Mrs. John Haysworth," or if the bride is not taking the groom's name "Mr. John Haysworth and Ms. Julia Phillips").

Timeless Traditions

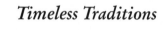

In parts of Africa, the broom represents the home. In eighteenth and nineteenth century America, slaves' weddings were not legally binding, so many couples jumped a broom as part of their ceremony in order to symbolize their entrance into married life. Many African-Americans carry on this tradition today.

ORDER OF SERVICE (JEWISH CEREMONY)

In most Jewish ceremonies, the order of service following the processional is as follows:

At the beginning of the ceremony, probably conducted in both Hebrew and English, the bride and groom sip the ceremonial wine and are blessed by the rabbi.

Exchange of rings.

The reading of the Ketubah, or marriage contract. The Ketubah belongs to the bride and outlines her rights in the marriage. The Ketubah is signed prior to the ceremony in the presence of the rabbi and two witnesses. In Orthodox ceremonies, only the groom signs the Ketubah, in reform or conservative ceremonies, the bride also signs.

A family member or very special guest recites the seven blessings. The bride and groom again sip the ceremonial wine.

The breaking of the glass. This ritual represents the destruction of the temple in Jerusalem; the guests shout "Mazel tov!" (good luck and congratulations). The glass should be wrapped for safety.

RECESSIONAL

CHRISTIAN CEREMONIES In Protestant ceremonies, the bride and groom exit first, then the maid/matron of honor (arm in arm with the best man), followed by the ring bearer and flower girl, and then the other attendants. The officiant then follows. If the bride's mother is seated with her husband, it is not necessary for a groomsman to come back up the aisle to escort her out. If the bride's father is in the wedding party or the bride's mother is not married or has no escort seated with her, a groomsman may be dispatched to escort her. The same applies to the groom's mother. Groomsmen/ushers may return to accompany grandmothers who are unescorted. They may also return to "release" the pews, although guests are generally well-mannered enough to know that the pews closest to the altar leave first, the pew closest to the door leaves last.

JEWISH CEREMONIES The bride and groom exit first, followed by the bride's parents, the groom's parents, grandparents, the honor attendants, the remaining attendants, the rabbi, and, lastly, the cantor.

The bride and groom then retire to a private place for a few minutes. By tradition, they should share their first meal together at this time, so generally a small plate of food is placed in the room for them. Christian brides and grooms should realize the soundness of this ritual and also take a moment together before the whirlwind of pictures followed by the reception, after which many couples complain "I never got anything to eat!"

Etiquette for Special Circumstances

SEATING FOR DIVORCED PARENTS

Generally the mothers sit in the front pew along with their new spouses, if applicable, and the fathers sit in the second pew with their wives, if applicable. If the bride or groom are closer to their fathers than their mothers, or if their stepmothers raised them, the fathers can certainly sit in the front. If relationships are good, there is no

---

Co-Ed Processionals

❧

***What happens to the processional if there are ladies on the
groom's side and/or gentlemen on the bride's?***

*It is not necessary for the bride to choose attendants from only her female friends or
for the groom to choose only among his male friends. The processional works in the
same manner as for evenly matched wedding parties except that if the bridesmaids
and groomsmen enter the church together, same sex pairs walk together but do not go
arm in arm.*

---

reason why parents, along with their spouses, shouldn't all sit in the
front row.

SEATING FOR EX-FAMILY MEMBERS

As though planning seating arrangements at the reception isn't
enough to drive couples over the brink of despair, it is now quite
common to find divorced parents complicating the ceremony by saying such things as "When we were married, that sister of yours did
nothing but try to break us up and now you're saying she's going to
sit in the same pew as my mother—over my dead body!" Notice to
feuding family members: Get over it. Since it is perfectly correct to
look solemn and not socialize unduly prior to a religious ceremony,
even archenemies should be able to manage sitting in the same pew

The Seating of Mothers and Grandmothers

❧

My fiancé and I are planning a wedding for June of next year and we have a couple of questions. As far as the seating of the mothers, what music do you recommend? Also, for the seating of the grandmothers—we have four—so who should be seated first? My two grandmothers? My fiancé's? Should they be seated according to age? Also, what music do you recommend for that? Should their corsages be all the same or should they vary? We're having a 2:00 P.M. ceremony and I want the mothers to wear long dresses. Should the grandmothers be in long dresses, too? Which grandmother should choose her dress/color first?

First of all, there is no such thing as an official "seating of the mothers." Your fiancé's mother should be seated second to last, your mother should be seated last, to whatever music you are planning for the prelude, unless, of course, your mother accompanies you up the aisle. The words "seating of the mothers," by the way, do not appear in the wedding program, or anywhere else for that matter. The "seating

without getting riled up. Family members who can't seem to get along with anybody else may whisper to the usher "Not in the first two rows please," and be done with it. Family members who just don't think that they'll be able to get through the day without starting arguments should recognize their shortcomings and stay home. It is not the bride or groom's responsibility to smooth over relationships, take sides, or endeavor to "patch things up" between family members.

of the grandmothers"? Well, that's quite a novel concept—and also a nonevent. What next? The "seating of the first cousins"? There is no rule as to which grand- mother is seated first nor should there be any jockeying for position—unseemly for any guest—much less for grandmothers. The very idea that any group of persons is seated at a wedding according to age is just too heinous to contemplate. The grandparents should be seated like any other guest, usually in one of the front two pews, depending on the size of your family and the size of the pews. If you choose to give the grandmothers corsages, they may be made up of any flower you wish. I don't recommend giving anyone but the mothers a corsage, but if you choose to make these ladies sport them, it would be charming to incorporate each grand- mother's favorite flower. If you're having a two o'clock ceremony, the mothers may not correctly wear long dresses. It stands to reason, therefore, that the grandmoth- ers do not wear long dresses either, nor are they compelled to choose any color over another. They may not wear black or white, that is all. I don't doubt that by the time ones' grandchildren are of marrying age one has a pretty good idea of what colors one likes or dislikes. Grandparents should be given their proper respect, not by being paraded up the aisle, but by being vigilantly introduced to guests at the reception and included in conversations during the same. Keep in mind that guests are only interested in the attendants' and the bride's trip up the aisle. Attempting to make a ceremony of anyone else's progress is tedious.

The Receiving Line

IF your guest count is not too large, you may wish to plan a receiving line at the church or synagogue immediately after the ceremony. Dis- cuss this with your officiant early on and if you plan to have the re- ceiving line outside, be sure to have a backup plan in case of inclement weather. (See chapter 14 for more information on the receiving line at the ceremony site.)

Music for the Ceremony

AT church/synagogue weddings, the musical director will generally provide you with guidelines for your musical selections. You should work closely with this person regarding your preferences, since some music may not be appropriate for your ceremony based on religious restrictions (there is no music at Orthodox Jewish or Quaker weddings) and many musical directors prefer that you use in-house rather than outside musicians. Some Catholic churches, for instance, will not allow "Bridal Chorus" from Wagner's Lohengrin because it is a secular, not religious piece and many synagogues discourage it because the composer was an anti-Semite. If your wedding takes place outdoors, your musicians must be forewarned, they will require a tent in the event of very warm or inclement weather. It is not necessary to invite ceremony musicians to the wedding reception.

SUGGESTIONS FOR THE PRELUDE

Handel: *Water Music* ("Air"), "Concerto Grosso in D Major," "Op.3, no. 6" (*Vivace*), "Aria from the Tenth Organ Concerto"

Bach: "Air on the G String," "Jesu Joy of Man's Desiring," "Bist du bei mir," "Sinfonia" (from Cantata No. 156), "Violin Concerto No.2 in E Major" (allegro assai), "Air from Suite in D for Strings"

Schubert: "Serenade"

SUGGESTIONS FOR THE BRIDE'S PROCESSIONAL

Wagner: "Bridal Chorus" (from *Lohengrin*)

Clarke: "Prince of Denmark's March: Trumpet Voluntary"

Pachelbel: "Canon in D"

Mozart: "Wedding March" (from *The Marriage of Figaro*)

Vivaldi: *The Four Seasons* ("Winter," "Largo")

Purcell: "Trumpet Tune and Air"

SUGGESTIONS FOR DURING THE CEREMONY

Schubert: "Ave Maria"

Bach: "Ave Maria," "Arioso," "Sheep May Safely Graze"

Hadel: "Hallelujah Chorus" (from *Messiah*)

For the congregation to sing

"Joyful, Joyful We Adore Thee"

"Love Divine, All Loves Excelling"

"All Things Bright and Beautiful"

"Dodi Li"

"Jerusalem of Gold"

"Shalom Alechem"

For the Recessional

Widor: "Touata" (from *Symphony No. 5*)

Elgar: "Pomp and Circumstance"

Medelssohn: Wedding March (from *Midsummer Night's Dream*)

Civil Ceremonies

A civil ceremony may be a simple trip to city hall or to the offices of a justice of the peace, or it may be an elaborate affair held in a ballroom

(continues on page 166)

Vow Renewal Ceremonies

❧

My husband and I have been married for fifteen years and have two children, ages thirteen and ten. We were married in a very short, informal civil ceremony, which was all our budget would allow. We now would like to reaffirm our vows. How should invitations be worded? Do we register for gifts (we did not fifteen years ago)? I was married in a suit the first time; now that I can afford whatever I like, is it appropriate for me to wear a veil? How should we include our children? Should I have bridesmaids?

Renewal of vows is a charming idea, usually done in celebration of an anniversary. A renewal of vows allows your children, and the close friends you have gathered during the course of your marriage, to witness your commitment. It's also lovely to include those who attended your wedding, especially if you have fallen out of touch (rather than fallen out of friendship), in order to rekindle old ties. Invitations to a vow renewal ceremony do not have to comply with the stricter standard of a wedding invitation. I suggest:

Jane and David Doe
invite you
to attend
their vow renewal ceremony
on
Saturday, the tenth of June
two thousand
at half after four o'clock ...

Your children should stand with you during the ceremony, should participate in the ceremony, and be mentioned during the ceremony by name. A renewal of vows not only reaffirms your commitment as a couple but also as a family. Since you are not a bride, but rather a wife, it's impossible for you to have bridesmaids. And even though you missed the opportunity to register for gifts fifteen years ago, you may not do so now. After the fifteen anniversaries, thirty birthdays, and possibly fifteen Christmases that you and your husband have shared (giving you a total of sixty gift-giving opportunities), I hazard that if you don't have it by now, you don't need it. You may not, however, put "No Gifts Please" on your invitation. Instead, you must spread, via word of mouth, that the only gifts you wish to receive are the love and support of those closest to you. If any guests do bring gifts, they should never be opened in front of other guests nor displayed on a "gift table." Gifts should be opened in private and followed by a sincere, handwritten, prompt, thank you. A vow renewal celebration should not be viewed as an opportunity to out-do your first wedding, even if you can now afford to. Unless you wish to renew your vows in your original gown, you may not wear a wedding dress with all the trimmings. Follow, instead, the guidelines for a second marriage—which means no train and no veil. You may wear whatever color you like, including white, and your clothing should be appropriate to the time of day and the formality of the occasion.

Above all, it should be clear to all those involved that you are renewing your vows as a way to publicly share your commitment with renewed vigor. Care should be taken that no one feels as though you are trying to throw yourself a second wedding, complete with all the trappings, without the bittersweet achievement of a second marriage.

(continued from page 163)

with many guests. The ceremony is not performed by a religious figure, although it will undoubtedly contain many spiritual elements. Couples whose different religions prohibit their being married in a religious ceremony or whose preference dictates it may chose a civil ceremony. Some time after the civil ceremony, there may be religious ceremony during which the union is blessed. A civil ceremony may allow more freedom than a religious ceremony as far as music and readings, although the solemnity of the occasion should be a priority and frivolous additions to the ceremony should be avoided. Recessional music, however, can be lots of fun. I have a friend whose recessional, performed instrumentally, was the Simon and Garfunkle classic "Feelin' Groovy."

Double Ceremonies

VERY often double ceremonies celebrate the marriage of two sisters, two very close cousins, or less often, two very close friends. (See chapter 6 on how to issue invitations to a double ceremony.) As in the wording of the invitations, the older sister precedes the younger. When the grooms assemble at the altar with their attendants, the older sister's groom stands closest to the officiant, his best man on his left, then the younger sister's groom with his best man on his left. The processional unfolds slightly differently than in a single wedding. The older sister's and her groom's attendants proceed up the aisle (either in single file or paired), followed by the older sister on her father's arm. Following that, the younger sister's and her groom's attendants

Timeless Traditions

*S*till done in some places, particularly Great Britain, "banns" or the couple's intention to marry were posted and read over a 21-day period in church. This gave anyone who objected to the union time to come forward.

proceed, followed by the younger sister escorted by a close male relative. The first couple assembles at the left side of the altar, the second couple on the right. The brides' father stands closest to the eldest daughter while the younger bride's escort sits in a front pew. Following the service, the older sister and her husband go down the aisle first, followed by their attendants, followed by the younger sister and her husband, followed by their attendants.

SEATING FOR A DOUBLE WEDDING

If space permits, the families of both grooms should be seated on the first pew on the right. If space does not permit, the family of the groom of the older daughter sits in the first pew; the other family sits in the second pew.

Military Weddings

ANY enlisted man or woman may have a military ceremony. Ladies and/or gentlemen may wear full dress uniform. Men in uniform do not wear boutonnieres. During the recessional, an arch is created out of drawn swords and the couple passes beneath it. Also, the wedding cake is cut with the groom's sword. (See chapter 6 for wording on invitations to a military wedding.)

Etiquette for Friends and Guests

PLANNING a wedding ceremony does not involve the input of friends and guests; the couple's own wishes and their religion's(s') guidelines dictate the type of ceremony they have. Discussions about religion and

Dos & Don'ts

❧

Do ask lots of questions when you first meet with your officiant.

Do attempt to incorporate both religions if you are having an interfaith ceremony.

Do try to steal a few minutes alone with each other after the ceremony.

Do have a backup if you plan to have a receiving line outside the church.

Do treat a civil ceremony as a serious occasion.

Do include your children in vow commitment ceremonies.

Don't hire an officiant that either you or your fiance are uncomfortable with.

Don't ask the best man to double as an usher; he has too much to do already.

Don't let family squabbles over seating arrangements spoil your planning process.

Don't make grandparents wait to be seated.

Don't attempt to make a ceremony over mothers being seated.

its merits or drawbacks should be avoided during the ceremony-planning process. Friends and guests whose beliefs are in sharp contrast with those of the bride or groom's religion should exercise the religious freedom to which they are entitled and pipe down.

9

IMMEDIATELY FOLLOWING . . .

ETIQUETTE FOR PLANNING THE RECEPTION

OVER THE PAST twenty years or so, wedding receptions have become more and more extravagant, even for brides and grooms with fairly ordinary means. The wedding cake, champagne, and finger-sandwich receptions of the past have all but disappeared. Guests' expectations are quite a bit higher these days, too, but it's important to remember that although your guests are important, spending what you can afford is paramount. This chapter will address the most often asked reception-planning etiquette questions, from "Do I have to have a sit-down dinner?" to "Where do we seat divorced parents and ex-family members?" and "Should we have a full bar or just beer and wine?" The most beautiful wedding receptions reflect the joy of the bride and groom and their families, and as you begin your planning, try to keep things in perspective by realizing that your wedding reception has very little to do with your main objective—getting married.

Food—How Do We Know What to Expect?

❧

As much as my wife and I enjoy attending weddings, there is al-ways some element of confusion as to whether or what we're go-ing to be fed at the reception. We have two young daughters who are very picky eaters, and it would help considerably to know if we should feed them prior to going to the wedding or chance it and assume they'll be given a meal at the reception. The last wedding we went to started at 2:30 P.M., and at the re-ception, which started at 3:15 P.M., we were very disappointed to be served nothing but little tea sandwiches, petits fours, and wedding cake. The children (and my wife and I) were ravenous (and cranky) by the time we left, at 5:00 P.M.

I'm so pleased to hear that you enjoy attending weddings, those that do make the most delightful guests. I must tell you, however, that with weddings, as in the rest of life, it's unwise to assume anything. I urge you, therefore, to examine your in-vitations and corresponding envelopes in order to ascertain whether or not your two young children have actually been invited to these weddings. With that in mind, I'll help you figure out what you'll be getting to eat. A hostess is com-pelled to serve only two items at a reception: a drink with which to toast the bride and groom and a cake. That doesn't mean that I urge you to ward off impending crankiness by hitting the all-you-can-eat-buffet circuit prior to attending wed-dings. In addition to drink and cake, you can probably anticipate the following.

• Morning and lunchtime weddings are usually followed by a wedding break-fast, at which you can look forward to being served what is roughly the equivalent of Sunday brunch or lunch. This may include anything from pastries, omelets, or Belgian waffles to poached salmon or steamship round of beef.

* Late afternoon receptions correspond with tea, which is exactly what you described. No hostess wants to run the risk of serving anything more than "little tea sandwiches and petits fours" to guests who've already eaten lunch and have plans to go out (or home) to dinner after the reception.

* Receptions that begin closer to the dinner hour will usually include much more substantial fare; a selection of heavy hors d'oeuvres including some that may be hot.

* Wedding receptions that begin at or after 6:00 P.M. will probably offer dinner, which could mean a full sit-down or buffet-style meal in addition to pre-dinner hors d'oeuvres.

Think of it. In a few years you and your wife will perhaps plan your own daughters' weddings. On those occasions you may serve whatever you like, all the while attempting to meet the substantial challenge of pleasing every guest (perhaps even those who were not invited) in addition to working within a budget. It's enough to make you lose your appetite, isn't it? It's best to attend weddings because you have a sentimental interest in at least one of the persons getting married, not because you expect a great spread. This makes disappointment so much easier to handle: "Pickled okra in aspic? Along with sautéed lamb kidneys? My favorite!" After having put such a brave face on the situation you may then whisper to your wife, "There's a phone downstairs, I'll make dinner reservations." Bon appétit!

Food

THERE is no reception food more correct than another: Barbecue in a renovated barn is as proper, albeit not as formal, as a five-course dinner in a hotel ballroom. The key to proper planning is to establish and stick to a degree of formality. If you've sent out engraved and formally worded invitations, don't surprise your guests with corn on the cob and hay bales at the reception. If you have the means to go "over the top" at your reception, go right ahead—have a sixteen-piece orchestra, caviar as an hors d'oeuvre, and lobster for dinner, as long as you or your parents normally entertain to that degree of lavishness. It is considered poor taste, however, to entertain guests in a manner that is clearly beyond one's means, not to mention bad financial planning.

THE PLATED OR SIT-DOWN DINNER

The most formal evening receptions usually begin with a cocktail hour followed by a plated (sit-down) dinner. The cocktail hour usually includes butlered hors d'oeuvres, which means they are arranged on platters and passed (along with a napkin) to each guest, as opposed to their being placed on a table for guests to help themselves. The hors d'oeuvres prior to a plated dinner should be light. Four different hors d'oeuvres for every hour of the cocktail hour provide plenty of choice for your guests. The hors d'oeuvres should be easy to eat in one bite and not overly messy. A restaurant-sized egg roll slathered in duck sauce is nothing but trouble for ladies and gentlemen in evening clothes. Keep in mind that many people have dietary restrictions, no shellfish or pork for religious reasons, for instance, and vegetarians must be considered also. You may, of course, choose a deliberate theme for all the food—Italian, French or Vietnamese, perhaps—especially if the country's cuisine reflects your own cultural heritage. When choosing ethnic cuisine, try not to alienate guests by completely eschewing popular dishes in favor of those no one has ever heard of. At a plated dinner, guests may sit down to find their first course already on the table, or it may be served to them. These days it is rare to see more than three courses, although more is of course correct. One may give guests a choice between two entrées and let them order as they would in a restaurant, but, since this is costly and slows service, one also may serve two (smaller) entrées on one plate. As a courtesy, you should ask your banquet manager or caterer to prepare several entrées for those guests you know don't eat meat and a few extras for unexpected vegetarians. Here are two sample menus for a cocktail hour followed by a plated dinner:

MENU 1
Cocktail Hour

Jumbo Gulf Shrimp with Horseradish Cocktail Sauce
Miniature Beef Tenderloin Satays
Bruschetta Topped with Tomatoes and Olive oil
Miniature Quesadillas with Grilled Chicken and Cilantro

Very Formal Dinner

Consommé
Poached Salmon with Hollandaise Sauce (fish course)
Filet Mignon of Beef (meat course)
Potatoes Anna
Baby Carrots
Wild Greens Salad (in formal dining, the salad
comes at the end of the meal)
Wedding Cake

MENU 2
Cocktail Hour

Miniature Crab Cakes with Rémoulade Sauce
Sliced Bosc Pears wrapped in Prosciutto
Vegetable Dumplings with Ginger-Soy Dipping Sauce
Artichoke Hearts stuffed with Danish Fontina

Formal Dinner

Oysters Rockefeller
Petite New Zealand Lamb Chops and Roasted Salmon "Mignon"
Roasted Fingerling Potatoes
Green Beans with Caramelized Leeks and Chanterelles
Wedding Cake

The first dinner menu is quite formal, quite correct, but rarely seen today. Additions such as a sorbet "intermezzo" dessert course and cheese course can be added to either menu if you'd like.

THE PLATED LUNCHEON

Formal daytime receptions should include a sit-down lunch. There may be a cocktail hour, but with fewer and lighter hors d'oeuvres. For example:

Cocktail Hour

Onion and Sage Tartlets
Sesame Shrimp Toasts
Miniature Cucumber Sandwiches with Dill Cream Cheese

Luncheon

Spinach Salad with English Stilton and Raspberry Vinaigrette
Chicken Breasts stuffed with Goat Cheese and Basil
Penne with Tomatoes, Pesto, and Artichokes
Wedding Cake

Serving chicken at any meal, by the way, is quite correct. Diana, the late Princess of Wales, served it at her wedding reception, as did the late Mrs. Jacqueline Onassis.

THE BUFFET MEAL

Buffet meals may be served at any time of day and are considered less formal than the sit-down dinner. They may or may not be preceded by a cocktail hour. Buffet meals are usually set on long tables with rounds often placed in between. Since all hot foods must be kept in chafing dishes, it's important to choose items that hold up well to long periods of heating. Chef-attended stations are a popular addition to the buffet meal and, since the entrées are prepared to order your menu will be afforded greater flexibility. These stations lend themselves well to ethnic cuisines: sushi stations, quesadilla stations, and stir-fry stations are all popular. Seating tables may be preset with silverware for the buffet dinner, or guests may pick up their silverware, usually wrapped in a napkin, at the end of the buffet. You may also choose for your first course to be pre-set at seating tables with the main course served buffet style. A good buffet-style menu should provide plenty of choices.

DINNER
Chef Attended Station 1

Penne or Fettuccine with Carbonara, Alfredo,
or Plum Tomato Sauce
Smoked Chicken Sausage
Prosciutto
Shrimp
Mushrooms
Basil
Red Peppers
Asparagus
Parmesan Cheese
Foccacia with Flavored Olive Oils for Dipping

Chef Attended Station 2

Roasted Filet of Beef
Leg of Lamb
Turkey Breast
Marsala Cream Sauce
Mustard Chive Sauce
Mint Sauce
Red Wine Pan Gravy

Placed on the Buffet Table

Caesar Salad with Garlic Croutons
Grilled Vegetables with Garlic and Olive Oil
Potato and Gorgonzola Gratin
Wedding Cake

Brunch
Chef-Attended Station 1

Omelets and crepes with crabmeat, sliced chicken breast, bacon,
smoked salmon, Gruyère, Cheddar cheese, mushrooms,
green peppers, spinach, chives, and béchamel Sauce

Chef-Attended Station 2

Banana Bread French Toast with strawberry, blueberry,
and apple compotes; walnuts, whipped cream, and maple syrup

Placed on the Buffet Table

Potatoes O'Brien
Fresh Fruit Salad
Assorted Muffins, Scones, and Biscuits
Jams, Marmalades, and Butter
Wedding Cake

Luncheon
Chef-Attended Station 1

Baked Ham and Prime Rib of Beef
Assorted Rolls and Breads
Flavored Mayonnaises and Mustards

Chef-Attended Station 2

Sautéed Shrimp
Creamy Stoneground Grits
Tasso Ham

Andouille Sausage
Sharp Cheddar Cheese
Jalapeño Jack Cheese
Lime Butter

On the Buffet Table

Green Bean and Red Onion Salad with Balsamic Vinaigrette
Roasted Red Skin Potatoes with Garlic, Olive Oil, and Cilantro
Orzo with Feta Cheese, Olives, and Tomatoes
Wedding Cake

HEAVY HORS D'OEUVRES BUFFETS

IF your wedding does not coincide with a mealtime, you should consider serving heavy hors d'oeuvres. Hors d'oeuvres buffets need not be as elaborate as dinner buffets; one or two substantial items along with several lighter items should suffice. For example:

Filet of Beef and Pork Tenderloin with Rolls, Croissants,
Flavored Mayonnaises and Mustards
Spinach and Artichoke Dip with Baguette Slices
Miniature Smoked Trout and Crab Cakes with
Cucumber Tartar Sauce
Mushroom-Stuffed Brie en Croûte
Crudités with an assortment of Dipping Sauces
Wedding Cake

BUTLERED HORS D'OEUVRES

If your reception does not coincide with a mealtime and space is at a premium, you can do away with buffet tables all together and have the hors d'oeuvres butlered. Be sure to combine a selection of hot and cold hors d'oeuvres and offer at least four selections for every hour of your reception. Keep in mind that when you select any menu it's almost impossible to please every single guest. By the same token, don't just stick to serving what you like. Remember that you and the groom are only two people on your guest list, and it's unfair to deny people shrimp just because you hate it.

METHODS OF SERVICE
The sit-down dinner can be served in several ways, all of which are correct.

BANQUET STYLE Servers, usually four for an eight-person table or one server per two guests, carry two plates of food each. They surround the table, serve the first of their two guests and then the second. They clear plates in the same manner. Usually each table or two is assigned a water and wine server whose only job is to keep beverages replenished.

Á LA RUSSE Servers bring the food to the table in serving dishes. The food is presented to each guest, who then helps himself.

FAMILY STYLE A charming and intimate way to have a sit-down dinner without the cost of added service staff. Plattered food is placed on the tables and guests serve themselves. This method of service, though quite informal, does eliminate long buffet lines and also encourages conversation and interaction among guests, even if it just starts out "Would you please pass the béarnaise sauce?"

SETTING THE TABLE
For the most formal dinners a service plate or charger should always be used and the first course should be set on that plate. A clean plate

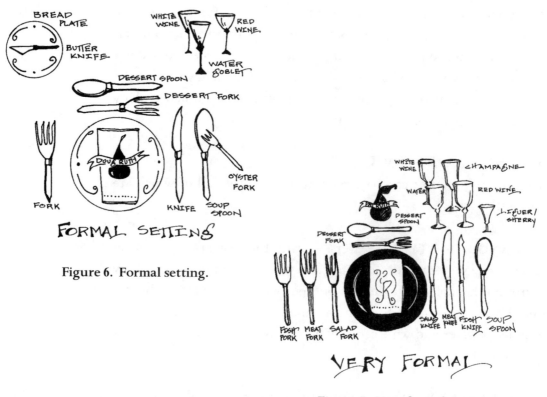

Figure 6. Formal setting.

Figure 7. Very formal setting.

should replace a used one with each course. This type of service is only seen at the most formal dinners these days. Figures 6 and 7 show service for formal and very formal dinners.

Note that there is no butter plate or knife in the most formal service. For very formal dinners bread is eaten off the tablecloth, not a plate, and butter is never served. Also note that there isn't a coffee cup or saucer on the tables. Servers should bring the cups and saucers on trays after dinner, providing them to guests who indicate that they'd like coffee.

As previously mentioned, a buffet dinner table may be pre-set with silverware, a napkin, bread with a bread plate and butter knife,

Figure 8. Setting for buffet dinner.

and a water goblet (see figure 8). (For a thorough discussion of table decorations, including linens and flowers, please see chapter 10.)

The Wedding Cake

THE wedding cake is an essential part of any wedding reception. The style and flavor of the cake is dictated by fashion therefore individual wedding cakes or cupcakes layered to resemble a wedding cake are just as correct as a traditional multitiered all white cake. The following are the most common types of icings:

FONDANT ICING

Made from sugar, corn syrup, gelatin, and glycerin, this type of icing is rolled out, like pastry, then applied to each tier of the cake. The resulting look is exceptionally clean and smooth, although not necessarily delicious.

BUTTERCREAM/CREAM CHEESE ICING

Made from butter or cream cheese and confectioner's sugar, this is probably the best tasting icing. However, because the butter or cream cheese base does not stand up well to heat, this icing is not a good choice for cakes that are going to be exposed to heat—at a summer outdoor reception, for instance. Buttercream or cream cheese frosting can be flavored and also used as a filling between cake layers.

ROYAL ICING

This icing, though soft when applied to a cake, dries to a very hard, smooth finish. Generally this icing is used for decoration, as opposed to a frosting for the whole cake.

GUM PASTE, MARZIPAN, AND SPUN SUGAR ICING

Gum paste is used to create extremely lifelike flowers and decorations; it dries to a very hard finish. Marzipan is made from ground almonds, sugar, and egg. Like fondant, it can be rolled into sheets. More often, however, it is colored with food coloring and made into realistic looking sugared fruits. Spun sugar is caramelized sugar that is spun into airy, tulle-like shapes. Like buttercream, spun sugar melts easily.

Wedding Day Reflections

I'd saved the top layer of my cake, painstakingly covered in plastic wrap and frozen, for my first-year anniversary. One morning after a particularly late night my husband remarked "When I came in from work last night, I was so hungry and tired, I didn't even feel like opening a can of soup, but did you know there was this little cake in the freezer? I defrosted it and ate it for dinner. Where did you get it? It was great!" So much for the anniversary.

—Cathy

The Groom's Cake

THE groom's cake was often sliced and given to guests to take home as a favor. Today the groom's cake often celebrates the groom's hobbies or personal interests. Fly fishermen may have a cake in the form of a trout; sports fans may choose their favorite team's mascot. The possibilities are endless; flavored frostings and cakes are popular, and although rare for a wedding cake, chocolate is a favorite for the groom's cake. The cake needn't be given as favors, although that is still correct. It may be sliced after the wedding cake and offered as a dessert option.

The Bar

THE bar, aside from seating arrangements, often creates the greatest degree of wedding reception planning controversy. Know that it is every bit as correct *not* to serve alcohol as it is to have a full bar, especially if the reception is held in the morning or early afternoon. If one family disapproves of drinking alcohol, but the other does not, compromise must be achieved early on. Perhaps the wedding can be "dry" with champagne served only for toasting. Perhaps a cocktail such as a kir royal (champagne and Chambord, a raspberry liqueur) can be served to drinkers while a nonalcoholic equivalent (sparkling cider or grape juice with raspberry syrup) can be offered to nondrinkers. If the wedding is to be "dry," there's no need to forewarn guests. Guests who find out that the reception is "dry" should kindly show respect and not turn up with hip flasks.

Timeless Traditions

Originally, the top layer of the wedding cake, traditionally a dark fruitcake covered in almond paste and iced with royal icing, was saved then used as a christening cake. After the wedding the almond paste and icing were removed, the cake wrapped in cheesecloth soaked in brandy for the requisite nine months, give or take a few months, then re-iced and decorated. Today many brides and grooms plan to save the cake for their one-year anniversary. Unfortunately, this practice lacks practicality simply because, other than the now extremely unpopular fruitcake, cakes do not last for a year in the freezer. If you want to save your top layer, eat it on your three-month anniversary.

FULL BAR

Full bar generally includes the following types of liquors, beers, and wines: vodka, gin (along with vermouth for martinis), bourbon, Scotch, white wine (usually chardonnay or sauvignon blanc), red wine (usually merlot, pinot noir, cabernet sauvignon, or zinfandel), champagne, and light and regular beer. Other liquors such as tequila or single-malt whiskeys may be added, along with liqueurs such as Kahlúa, Grand Marnier, Bailey's, and cognac. Standard mixers are regular and diet cola, lemon-lime soda, tonic water, soda water, ginger ale, and cranberry, orange, and grapefruit juices. Garnishes typically include maraschino cherries, olives, lemons, and limes. If the meal is to be sit down, wines are poured for each course, during which time the bar may or may not remain open. In the event that the bars close during dinner, guests should realize that the wines have been chosen to specifically complement the food and they should not attempt to coerce bartenders or servers into getting them "another white Russian" to drink with the Dover sole. If there is to be dancing after dinner, the bars reopen.

Timeless Traditions

It was traditional to toast the bride and groom with champagne simply because champagne was considered the quintessential celebration drink and often was the only alcohol served at the reception. You may serve champagne throughout your reception, or only for toasting, although it is necessary to provide an alternative (sparkling cider perhaps) served in a champagne glass, to nondrinkers. It is not unacceptable to eliminate champagne altogether and simply ask guests to toast with whatever they're drinking. The toast is a requirement, the champagne is not.

BEER AND WINE BARS

Beer and wine bars need only include a red and white wine and light and regular beers along with soft drinks. Champagne may be poured at the bar, or reserved for toasting only. It is not necessary to include fruit juices among the mixers, although it's a nice touch. If you feel there will be many nondrinkers or children at the reception, it's also nice to include a nonalcoholic punch at the bar.

THEME BARS

As with reception food, the bar is largely dictated by fashion, and right now it's very popular to include theme bars or theme drinks. You may have a martini bar, or a margarita bar, or simply serve one mixed drink, a cosmopolitan or a mint julep perhaps, along with a beer and wine bar. You may also have a wine-tasting bar with many varieties, or perhaps you would like to incorporate several beers made by a local microbrewery into your bar. All are perfectly correct under the following circumstances: Guests should never be offered alcohol without something to eat, particularly if you have a full liquor bar, and nondrinkers should always be offered something nonalcoholic in just as pretty a glass as the drinkers have and with just as many garnishes. The bar should close when your reception ends. Hosts do not schedule it to end an hour before the reception does in order to save money.

Wedding Day Reflections

My family does not drink, however, my fiancée and I do, as does her family. As a compromise, we had a "dry" rehearsal dinner and served alcoholic and nonalcoholic champagne cocktails at our wedding reception. It worked really well and no one came away feeling slighted.

—Josh

B.Y.O.B.

Guests do not pay for any of the reception. Asking them to "bring your own bottle" violates this rule and is a serious breech of etiquette.

GLASSWARE

The following types of glassware are all that are needed for even the most elaborate bar (see figure 9 for examples of each):

Figure 9. Glassware.

White wineglass, red wineglass, universal wineglass, brandy glass, champagne glass, beer pilsner, water goblet, martini glass, rocks glass liqueur or sherry glass,. A universal wineglass may be used in lieu of two wineglasses and a rocks glass can double as a water glass if you'd like.

Seating Arrangements

AT a sit-down dinner or at a full-meal buffet, there should be seating for each guest. Less than this is acceptable only at receptions where the food is neither substantial nor difficult to eat, or where the food is butlered. In these cases there may be seating for most, but not all guests. While it is true that most people like to stand during a cocktail hour, few people are happy to eat pasta primavera with one hand and hold a drink in the other. Reserved seating should always be provided for older or pregnant guests and those who are able to stand comfortably should relinquish seats to those who cannot.

ASSIGNED TABLES AND ASSIGNED SEATS

As with seating during the ceremony, reception seating arrangements have less to do with etiquette than good manners and judgment. At a buffet or informal plated meal, guests may be assigned a table, but no specific seat. Prior to sitting down, guests pick up a seating card with their name and table number printed or written on it. Cards should be sorted alphabetically by last name; table numbers should be large enough to be readily seen. For more formal affairs, or if you simply would like more control over where guests are seated, you should provide assigned seating cards, which are generally placed above the dessert spoon and fork. If you go ahead with this type of seating plan, you must provide a seating chart, otherwise guests will wander aimlessly from table to table looking furtively for their name on the card. The chart needs simply to list the guests alphabetically with their table number next to the name along with a diagram of where the tables are placed. Again, table numbers should be clear. If your guest list is large, it's a good idea to have several seating charts made to avoid a bottleneck.

WHO SITS WHERE?

The bride's table usually consists of the bride and groom and the wedding party (see figure 10 for example). A rectangular table is traditional but a round table appears to be far more intimate. The best man sits to the bride's right, the maid of honor sits on the groom's left. If there is room, the wedding party's spouses sit with them, if not, they may be seated at another table. Generally the minister and his or her

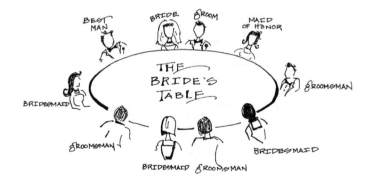

Figure 10. Bride's table.

Can We Charge for Liquor?

❧

I'm getting married in a month and people who've been invited keep asking me what's going to be served at the reception, particularly if there's going to be a full bar. After three months of discussion and compromise my parents, my fiancé, and I agreed on serving domestic beer and wine. I'm beginning to feel badly about not being able to afford to do more when so many people seem to expect it. Also, our resources limit us to being able to serve champagne for a toast only. During the past month, two of my relatives have said that they'd be willing to give us enough money to have a full bar. I'm really hesitant to accept. I've been to various charity events, where, in an effort to raise funds, they've sold tickets that can be subsequently exchanged for liquor drinks. What do you think of this idea?

First I would like to applaud you, your parents, and your fiancé for coming to a decision after three months of discussion and compromise. This approach is one that will enable you and your fiancé to one day say, "After fifty years of compromise and discussion, we've come to our golden anniversary." I hope that your invitees are not trying to ascertain whether or not the lavishness of your reception makes their attendance worthwhile, or worse, that they're basing their wedding-gift budget on the same premise. Perish the thought! That wouldn't be in the

spouse should be seated at the same table as the bride's parents. Family members should be seated together, particularly if they've traveled from many different locations and have a lot of catching up to do.

proper nuptial spirit now would it? When you're asked whether or not you'll be having a full bar, simply smile and say, "No, we thought it would be more fun to serve beer and wine." As kind as it is for your relatives to offer to throw in for a full bar, I caution you against accepting the proposition. Theoretically, your taking this money should give them no more authority than if they had no part in the financing. Backers, however, seldom relinquish control. What will you do when their idea of full bar turns out to be having bartenders prepare layered shooters for your toast while a master of ceremonies makes amusing commentary about your husband's college girlfriends? Objections to such merriment may be met with the refrain: "Why not? You know we are paying for it." Moreover, accepting such an offer will lay waste, at the eleventh hour, to your compromise. I suggest you thank your relatives profusely for their kind offer and consider it no more.

You can raise many things at a reception; a toast is one of them, money is not. Selling tickets or anything else at your reception is strictly prohibited. Serve only what you can afford; imaginative guests who drink nothing but bourbon and ginger ale will surely contrive a way to secure their preferred drink after the reception. It is also quite all right for champagne to be furnished for a toast only. If your reception style does not provide a seat and table space for everyone, leave plenty of time for champagne to be served. Being offered a champagne glass while clutching a buffet plate and a wineglass will seriously challenge even the most dexterous of guests.

Cheers!

Single guests should be seated with other single guests, married guests with other couples. If you are assigning seats, spouses should be seated at the same table but not next to each other. Older guests, or those who do not enjoy music, should be seated furthest away from the dance floor. Great care must be taken when assigning seating, especially for a plated meal. Table assignments should begin just as soon as RSVPs arrive.

FEUDING RELATIVES AND OTHER INEVITABILITIES

Obviously feuding relatives should be seated as far apart as possible, and never at the same table. Divorced parents should not be seated at the same table unless their relationship is exceptionally friendly. Family members and guests should not appeal to the bride and groom or their parents for special seating assignments. "I don't want to sit at Aunt Edith's table because she always criticizes my haircut" is not a problem that warrants a change in seating assignments. "I don't want to sit next to Aunt Edith because she always asks me loudly if I'm still a lesbian" does. At an assigned table or seat reception it's quite all right and inevitable for guests to move from their assigned tables in order to socialize with other guests after the meal is over and plates are cleared. Guests who don't like their seating assignment from the get go will respect their hosts' spending hour upon hour on the seating arrangements by not asking other guests to "switch."

LATE RSVPS AND SEATING

One of the most difficult aspects of assigned seating is that the arrangements cannot be completed until all RSVPs are accounted for. Tardiness and the RSVPs are inevitable, so it is logical to have an extra table for those who RSVP late or not at all. This table, due to its occupants' lack of consideration, is placed in the least favorable location in the room, next to the kitchen, for instance.

Entertainment

AT the most elaborate weddings, live music is provided. Often one group of musicians plays for cocktail hour, while another plays during the reception. At a reception that takes place in the same location as the wedding, ceremony musicians may be retained to play for cocktail hour while a band or DJ takes over for the reception. No type of music is more correct than another; if dancing is on the agenda music must be "danceable" for older and younger guests and not so loud that it overpowers the conversation and socializing intrinsic to wedding receptions. Lyrics should not be obviously obscene or overtly risqué. For receptions that do not include dancing, background music is correct whether performed by musicians or provided by a DJ. An effort should always be made to provide some music—CDs played on a portable stereo are just fine.

BANDS AND RIDERS

Generally a band or their booking agency will provide a client with a "rider," which outlines what the client must provide in order for the group to perform. Riders should be read carefully and complied with as much as possible. If your reception site is unable to accommodate, for instance, private dressing rooms as requested in a rider, it is your responsibility to inform the bandleader or booking agent. Bands usually have certain food and drink requirements that you should also make every effort to meet. It is not polite to sign a rider without intending to fulfill its requirements, not to mention that this may relieve the band of it's obligation to play, even if you've paid them in full. Your band or DJ is one of the key elements of your reception, to treat them with any less than the utmost deference and respect is a breach of good manners.

WHAT MUSICIANS WEAR

As a standard, bands and DJs wear black tuxedos or black dresses, although women lead singers rarely stick to black only. It is important that you make your dress code requirements clear and make sure that musicians are well aware of the reception's degree of formality.

MASTERS OF CEREMONIES

A recent and generally unnecessary addition to the reception, this role is generally played by the DJ. Aside from announcing the couple, introducing the best man's toast, and announcing the cutting of the cake, the bouquet toss, and the couple's leaving, there are really no other roles that need to be assigned to a master of ceremonies. Orchestrated "special" dances, suggestive commentary during the garter toss, and general chattiness should be avoided. If you do hire a DJ, be explicit about his or her role as a master of ceremonies.

Favors

ONCE a simple piece of boxed cake or a handful of Jordan almonds, favors, like much of the reception have become more elaborate. You may choose a theme for your favors—spring bulbs for a wedding at a botanical garden or fresh peaches at a summer wedding in the South, for instance. In any case, favors are a charming gesture if your means are ample, but they are not a requirement.

Etiquette for Friends and Guests

IT is an unfortunate and recent trend that finds guests offering planning advice to couples to ensure that the upcoming reception meets their own standards. "You've got to have a sit-down dinner" and "No

Dos & Don'ts

Do establish a degree of formality and stick to it.

Do serve hors d'oeuvres that are bite-sized and easy to eat.

Do offer guests something to eat whenever alcohol is served.

Do provide seating for every guest unless all the food is easy-to-eat hors d'oeuvres or butlered.

Do reserve seating for elderly or pregnant guests if you don't plan to have seating for everyone.

Do provide seating charts for assigned seat receptions.

Do make sure that table numbers are readily visible.

Do have an extra table for guests who RSVP late.

Do make an effort to provide some sort of music during your reception.

Do keep in mind that music is an essential part of your reception and that those who make it must be treated with respect; read entertainers' "riders" and adhere to their provisions.

Don't allow music to be so loud that those who don't want to dance are unable to socialize.

Don't serve only what you and the groom like.

Don't expect to save your wedding cake for a year. It won't last that long.

Don't allow masters of ceremonies to over-orchestrate your reception.

Don't feel obligated to give guests favors.

one will come if it's going to be dry" are statements cheerfully made by those neither planning nor paying for the reception. Guests who have had their own weddings may not use others' as an opportunity to fulfill their own "If I had to do it all again" aspirations. Those who have yet to be married can feel free to take mental or written notes to which they may refer when their turn rolls around. Guests kindly restrain themselves from calling the bride and groom to make special food requests. They have plenty to worry about without "Hey, this is Cindy. I just wanted to tell you that I'm on a wheat-, carbohydrate-, lactose-, and red-meat-free diet . . ." If you anticipate your dietary needs are not going to be met at the reception, eat before you go.

10

ROSES ARE RED . . .

ETIQUETTE FOR FLOWERS AND DECORATIONS

FLOWERS AND DECORATIONS are an enormously important part of the wedding and reception. Contrary to popular belief, flowers are not a "throw away" item—they last forever in your wedding photographs. This chapter will help couples make sense of floral and decorative quandaries, discern flower "meanings," and make the most of the flowers you choose, and will help you make the right decisions *before* you approach a florist or floral designer. (Please note that the terms "florist" and "floral designer" are used interchangeably in this chapter.)

Flowers

BECAUSE flowers are so important, not to mention costly, couples should educate themselves prior to embarking on decorating schemes.

THE BRIDAL BOUQUET

That the bride either wear or carry flowers or greenery is a rule of etiquette as old as weddings themselves. Whether you choose to carry an

What's Your Flower?

Flowers, rather like birthstones, are associated with certain months.

Month	Flower
January	Carnation
February	Violet
March	Jonquil
April	Sweet Pea
May	Lily of the Valley
June	Rose
July	Larkspur
August	Gladiola
September	Aster
October	Calendula
November	Chrysanthemum
December	Narcissus

armful of roses or a single blossom, nothing, aside from your dress, is as important to the look of your wedding as the flowers you select. Your choice of dress dictates your choice of flowers and floral designers usually won't schedule a consultation prior to your buying your dress and choosing the bridesmaids' dresses as well.

The most formal bride's bouquet, like the wedding cake, is traditionally white all through, and if the stems of the bouquet create its "handle," they are usually completely wrapped in ribbon.

BASIC BRIDAL BOUQUET SHAPES

Cascade: Flowers are arranged to fall forward in a waterfall effect.

Arm: Flowers are arranged to be held in the crook of the arm, like a baby.

Nosegay/Clutch: A small, rounded, upright shape, as though plucked from a vase. Once called a *colonial,* a large nosegay is the choice of many brides.

Free Form or Asymmetrical: As the name indicates, a loose collection of blooms gathered into an unconventional shape.

Pomander: A three-dimensional creation, often in the shape of a ball, carried by a loop of ribbon.

TYPES OF BOUQUET CONSTRUCTION

Wired: This means that most of a flower's actual stem is removed. A piece of wire is then threaded through the top of the existing stem and wound around it until it extends by itself. The resulting wired bloom can be twisted and turned to create the bouquet's shape. Wired bouquets are less heavy than hand-tied bouquets and their handles are much smaller.

Hand-Tied: The blooms are left on their own stems then tied together, usually with ribbon or tulle. The stems are also taped together prior to their being tied.

Composite: Individual petals or leaves are wired, then arranged together to create one giant blossom. This is an enormously time-consuming, and therefore expensive, method of creating a bouquet.

Assembled in Foam: Blooms are assembled in florists' foam, then placed in a plastic holder.

CHOOSING IN-SEASON BLOOMS

If you must carry lilacs in your bouquet, you must also get married in the spring—the only time of year they're available. The following list of seasonal and all-season flowers will help you with your planning.

In season all year:

Alstroemeria

Baby's Breath

Calla Lily

Carnation

Chrysanthemum

Daisy

Freesia

Gerbera Daisy

Gladiola

Iris

Ivy

Lily

Lisianthus

Roses

Smilax

Snapdragon

Stephanotis

Stock

Tuberose

Spring

Daffodil

Dianthus

Hyacinth

Hydrangea

Iceland Poppy

Lilac

Lily of the Valley

Peony

Summer

Cosmos

Phlox

Queen Anne's Lace

Sunflower

Sweet William

Yarrow

Zinnia

Fall

Cockscomb

Dahlia

Viburnum Berries

Winter

Amaryllis

Heather

Hellebores

Holly Berries

Narcissus

Poinsettia

The Meaning of Flowers

❧

Many flowers and herbs have meanings attached to their names. In Victorian times it was possible to conduct an entire romance through the giving and receiving of flowers. Even though couples now enjoy a more straightforward approach to communication and aren't stuck trying to make their point by dropping handkerchiefs and such, it's still fun to imagine that your bouquet can speak volumes.

Flower	Meaning	Flower	Meaning
Almond blossom	Sweetness, hope	Lily (white)	Purity
Amaryllis	Pride	Lily of the valley	Return to happiness
Bellflower (white)	Gratitude	Marigold	Joy
Bluebell	Constancy	Mint	Eternal refreshment
Carnation	First love	Orange blossom	Purity, loveliness
Chrysanthemum (red)	I love you	Peony	Bashfulness
		Pansy	Thinking of you
Daisy	Innocence	Rose (red)	Love
Dianthus	Divine love	Rosebud	Purity, loveliness
Forget-me-not	Fidelity, true love	Rosemary	Remembrance
Gardenia	Femininity	Snowdrop	Hope
Gladiola	Incarnation	Stephanotis	Marital bliss
Hibiscus	Delicate beauty	Stock	Lasting beauty
Ivy	Eternal fidelity	Tulip (red)	Declaration of love
Jasmine (white)	Amiability	Wallflower	Fidelity
Jasmine (yellow)	Elegance, happiness	Zinnia	Thinking of absent friends
Lavender	Devotion, virtue		

Hiring a Florist

EITHER a florist or floral designer can do a splendid job with your wedding flowers. Florists are vendors who create flower arrangements for delivery, pickup, and special events. They operate out of a retail space. Floral designers create flowers only for special events. They work out of a studio and are generally not open to the public for "walk ins." Select your vendor based on their reputation—for example, ask for the name of the designer the next time you see a magnificent centerpiece in a hotel or restaurant lobby. Caterers and event planners also are excellent sources for recommendations as are country clubs and hotels. A good floral designer will have plenty of photographs of their work to show you, and they should be receptive to ideas and photographs that you bring to them. Be sure to bring a picture of both your dress and the bridesmaids'; a swatch of fabric from both is also helpful. Keep in mind that the florist is a professional and knows a great deal more about flowers than you do. Rely on their good judgment and take their advice the way you that would a waiter's ("At this time of year, oysters aren't the best thing on the menu . . ."). Keep in mind that many wonderful photographs of flowers which appear in magazines are just that—photographs. In some instances flowers are designed to look gorgeous just for the photo shoot, but a duplicate of the bouquet may not stand up to the outdoor August

---

Wedding Day Reflections

*F*or my daughter's wedding I received two quotes from floral designers, one lower than the other. In an effort to save money, I chose the designer who'd submitted the lower bid. What a mistake! When I arrived at the ceremony/reception site an hour prior to the ceremony, the pale pink roses we'd ordered for the bouquets and centerpieces were already starting to brown. The composite rose we'd ordered for the cake topper was lopsided and two-tone instead of the one color we'd ordered. The metal arch for the ceremony was supposed to be

(continued)

wedding that you're planning. A good designer will understand the look you are attempting to achieve, however, and she will suggest substitutions if your choice of specific flowers proves to be impractical. Good designers will have a large selection of containers, candelabras, and props from which to choose, and, again, should grasp your vision early on, even if you don't know to call your look "English garden" or "clean, monochromatic, and modern."

Choosing the Appropriate Flowers

THE BRIDE'S BOUQUET

When choosing your bouquet, keep in mind the formality and location of your wedding and the style of your dress. A formal wedding, held at a church or synagogue, will require a formal bouquet, whereas an outdoor, informal wedding might be suited to a bouquet of loose wildflowers. If your dress is a ballgown style, don't choose a very large bouquet, the effect can be overwhelming. Tall brides are more likely to be able to pull off a large bouquet than petite brides, who may end up looking overpowered. All in all, a smaller bouquet made of premium blooms always outshines a large one made of ho-hum flowers. A family prayer book covered in flowers is a very traditional choice and an always-appropriate alternative to a bouquet. You may also wish to have flowers attached to your veil or placed in your

Wedding Day Reflections (continued)

completely covered in greenery and flowers; instead it had bare spots through which you could actually see the frame. All of these problems proved more obvious when we received our proofs from the photographer. The browned flowers spoiled many of the color shots; eventually we had to order hand-colored black and white pictures to replace the ruined colored ones. We took the florist to court and won enough money to cover the hand-coloring, but nothing can be done to truly replace the color photographs. In retrospect, I'd say that you really do get what you pay for.

—Barb

hair, both romantic options. Brides who opt for a short, civil ceremony may either carry a bouquet or choose a corsage instead.

BRIDESMAIDS' BOUQUETS

Bridesmaids' bouquets may match the bride's in color or flower type, or may be entirely different. If you have many bridesmaids or bridesmaids who will be wearing different colors, their bouquets should vary slightly. Perfectly matched bouquets, along with uniform dresses tend to create a stage-show effect, which is no longer fashionable. Bridesmaids needn't carry flowers; muffs for winter weddings or candles for evening weddings are both appropriate.

FLOWER GIRLS

If your site will allow it, the traditional choice is for flower girls to scatter petals on the aisle. Again, check with your site, many do not allow petals. Keep in mind, also, that rose petals can be very slippery. In lieu of rose petals, flower girls can carry pomanders, wreaths, baskets of flowers, or tiny nosegays; they can also wear flowers or wreaths in their hair.

FLOWERS FOR GENTLEMEN

The groom's boutonniere usually corresponds with one of the bridal bouquet's flowers, although it certainly may be different. If you have many groomsmen it makes sense to vary the boutonnieres slightly in order to alleviate a potentially boring look. In any case, boutonnieres should be small enough not to overwhelm or look clownish; roses, gardenias, stephanotis, and freesias are popular choices. If there are ushers in addition to groomsmen, they may also sport boutonnieres, although this is not necessary. The same applies to readers, soloists, and guest-book attendants. Generally, those who participate in the ceremony, along with the bride's and groom's fathers, should receive a boutonniere. Ring bearers may wear tiny boutonnieres if you wish.

FLOWERS FOR MOTHERS

Corsages, although always correct, have somewhat fallen out of fashion. Many mothers choose to carry small nosegays, which coordinate with, but do not exactly match, the bridesmaids' flowers. If you choose to give grandmothers flowers, by all means do so, but know that it is unnecessary, and that once you've started giving flowers to female relatives it can be difficult to draw the line.

Floral Decorations

FOR THE CEREMONY

Check with your church or synagogue to find out their flower restrictions, if any. Good designers should be familiar with many sites' restrictions and can help you avoid conflicts. If the site is large, altarpieces should be as big as you can afford and, in order to save money, made up of large flowers. If your wedding takes place in the evening, all-white altarpieces will stand out more than those made up of dark-colored or cool-colored (blue, lavender, or purple) flowers, which tend to "disappear" in low light. Aisle markers, floral arches, decorated candelabras, door wreaths, and other decorations are lovely—if your budget will accommodate them. If your budget is small, concentrate more on your reception flowers; after all, your guests may spend only thirty minutes at the ceremony, but possibly three hours or more at the reception.

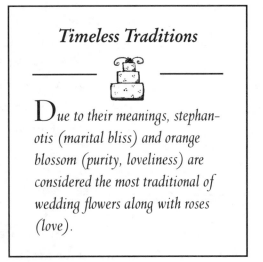

Timeless Traditions

Due to their meanings, stephanotis (marital bliss) and orange blossom (purity, loveliness) are considered the most traditional of wedding flowers along with roses (love).

FOR THE RECEPTION

The rule of etiquette for centerpieces is that they be tall enough or short enough not to hinder anyone's vision. Nothing inhibits your guests' socializing more than huge eye-level centerpieces, no matter how gorgeous. If your reception is large and you have many tables, vary your centerpieces. Different heights, different containers, different flowers of the same color, or the same flowers in different colors help prevent a boring, overly uniform look. Although an all-white color scheme is the favorite of many brides, keep in mind that white centerpieces on white linens tend to get lost. If you are having an evening reception, include plenty of candlelight on your tables. Candlelight lives, breathes, and moves and nothing else creates such a romantic (and relatively inexpensive) look. Professional lighting can create a truly stunning look for your reception. It is, however, prohibitively expensive for many brides.

CAKE FLOWERS

Traditionally, the cake table is decorated with the bridesmaid's bouquets along with the bride's if she wishes. If you order a cake design that includes fresh flowers, be sure to establish who will provide the flowers—your florist or your baker. Since the flowers on your cake will be out of water be sure to choose edible, unsprayed flowers that hold up well for an extended period of time. Petals scattered on the cake table look lovely and are less costly than whole flowers.

Linens

LINENS are an important factor in your overall reception look and should not be neglected. If you are having your reception at a hotel or country club or at another facility that provides its own linens, find out exactly the type, color, and quality of linens that are included. It is not necessary for table linens to match the color of your bridesmaids' dresses. In fact, a lot of one color can look too contrived and over-whelming. The color of the linens should, however, compliment your overall color scheme. Many facilities only provide lap-length linens in white or ivory, and while this does suffice, linens that reach the floor are infinitely more formal and elegant. Generally, the facility will charge you extra to upgrade to longer or colored linens, or they may allow you to rent them yourself. Many floral designers carry beautiful linen selections; rental companies also have a wide array from which to choose. Your caterer may also provide or rent beautiful linens for you, again, at an additional cost. You may also wish to rent chair covers, especially if your hotel or country club's chairs do not fit your color scheme. Flowers attached to the back of chairs are a lovely touch, particularly on the chairs at an outdoor wedding.

The Tossing Bouquet

USUALLY ordering a special bouquet just for tossing is an unnecessary expense. Unless you're planning to have your bouquet preserved (in which case it should be put in water as soon as possible), or if it is very large and heavy, there is no reason not to toss it. I realize that brides are loath to part with their flowers, but I assure you, after four hours out of water, even the most fabulous bouquet will look tired and limp. It's difficult to justify the extra cost of a tossing bouquet when you'll end up keeping the "real" bouquet for at most only one night before throwing it away when you leave for your honeymoon.

Tossing Petals

ROSE petals tossed as the bride and groom leave the reception are very romantic and create wonderful photographs, particularly if it's dark and the petals are white. Unless you're sure that every single guest will remain for the goodbye, don't order petals for more than 50% of your total guest count. Again, check with your site to be sure they allow petal tossing, or to find out if they charge an extra fee for cleanup. Petals can be placed in individual cones for tossing, or they can be piled into a basket from which each guest can remove a handful.

Etiquette for Friends and Guests

UNLESS the bride has specifically asked you to take home the table decorations, kindly refrain from removing them or demolishing buffet centerpieces like a swarm of locusts. The bride may have chosen to have her flowers donated to a hospital, or delivered to shut-ins, or given to charity. She may also have asked specific friends or guests to take them home. Centerpiece containers are sometimes rented or may belong to the floral designer, and she'll lose her deposit if they disappear. Friends and relatives who receive corsages or boutonnieres should not complain about having to wear them. Those who do not receive them should please refrain from throwing hissy fits due to the (intentional or unintentional) oversight.

Wedding Day Reflections

I *really wasn't interested in traditional centerpieces for my wedding reception tables. Instead I rented gorgeous chocolate-colored crushed-velvet linens from my floral designer. On the tables were tall vases filled with water and rose petals, topped by floating candles. Around the vases, I chose scattered rose petals surrounded by lots of small votive candles; the effect was stunning.*

—Lynne

Dos & Don'ts

🌹

Do choose your dress and bridesmaids' dresses prior to meeting with a florist.

Do bring fabric swatches, if possible, to the meeting.

Do select formal bouquets if you're planning a formal wedding.

Do obtain references prior to choosing a florist.

Do take your designer's advice about flowers; remember, she's the expert.

Do be willing to accept flower substitutions if your designer recommends them for the best look.

Do use lots of candlelight at an evening reception.

Do make sure your linens fall to the floor for the best look.

Do check with your site to make sure that tossing petals is allowed.

Do remember that, as with other wedding-related items, you get what you pay for.

Don't feel all your bridesmaids and groomsmen's flowers have to match exactly.

Don't feel obligated to provide all your female relatives with flowers.

Don't use dark or cool-colored flowers for an evening reception.

Don't choose centerpieces that block guests' vision across the table.

Don't spend the extra money on a tossing bouquet unless you plan to have yours preserved.

11

HOLD THAT POSE

ETIQUETTE FOR PHOTOGRAPHY AND VIDEOGRAPHY

PHOTOGRAPHY AND VIDEOGRAPHY is expensive, and agreeing with parents on the style of the finished product can be challenging. Achieving a balance between two families' and many individuals' expectations might be difficult, but is certainly possible. This chapter will help you know what to expect from your photographer and videographer as well what they expect from you. It will help you to answer questions such as: "Do I have to have a formal portrait?," "How long will the photography take after the ceremony?," and "Am I responsible for feeding the videographer?" Your photographs and video are, in addition to your own memories, everlasting. It is imperative that they measure up to your standards.

Types of Photographers

BEFORE you schedule a meeting with a photographer, you should ascertain which styles of photography best suit your taste.

TRADITIONAL

Traditional photographers create posed images with very few candid or action shots.

PHOTOJOURNALISTIC

Although photographers of this type do shoot group, posed pictures, they rely on an unobtrusive, unposed, unorchestrated approach to most of the photography.

COMMERCIAL

Commercial photographers will take pictures of your cake, flowers, food, and decorations that will look like they came straight from the pages of a magazine. If this is a priority for you, you should also hire another photographer to take photographs of the people in and at your wedding.

Hiring a Photographer

As with other wedding vendors, the very best photographers book quickly for popular dates, so begin your search for a photographer just as soon as you become engaged. When you meet with a photographer, you should be shown plenty of her work. Keep in mind, though, that she is only going to show you the very best shots, from the loveliest weddings, of the prettiest brides. In addition to images of weddings and receptions, your photographer should show you bridal portraits as well as engagement pictures. It is extremely important that you establish a good rapport with your photographer. She will be with you for many hours on your big day and will make many demands on your time and probably your patience. It is important that the photographer's style matches the one you like the best. Make sure that your parents have a say in this, too. If your mother is steadfastly traditional and your idea of a great wedding portrait is you, barefoot in your dress, standing in a field of wildflowers, you might want to think about hiring two photographers—traditional and artistic. You may be able to get away with just one photographer if she is willing and able to shoot two different styles of picture. Just make sure that she is aware of both your and your mother's visions. If your guest list and wedding party are very large, your photographer will require an assistant; don't try to circumvent this recommendation, it may be the only way you'll be sure to get complete coverage of your day.

COLOR VERSUS BLACK AND WHITE

Most brides prefer a mix of black and white and color; be sure to tell your photographer what percentage of each you'd prefer. Many photographers shoot two types of black and white, one sharp and one grainy. Ascertain which you prefer and also ask about other types of film, such as infrared (if you like this look), and whether she has enough cameras to shoot several types of film at once.

THE PACKAGE DEAL

Most photographers price their work according to the number of hours you wish them to cover and how many rolls of film they'll use. Usually their pricing includes the proofs, as well as albums in some cases, or album consultations. Be sure to find out who wants what before signing a package deal. The groom's parents should be consulted, and you'll need to talk to your parents about whether or not they'll be paying for albums or prints for in-laws, grandparents, and other relatives. Be realistic about the amount

Timeless Traditions

It is a tradition, especially in the South, to display the bride's formal portrait at the reception. Many brides are amending this practice by displaying a small black and white portrait (no larger than 8 1/2 by 11 inches) on a table, rather than an easel, along with her parents', grandparents', and in-laws' wedding portraits.

of time you expect the photographer to work. Most will begin taking pictures an hour prior to the ceremony's starting, so hours can add up if you want her to stay until the end of the reception. Ask when you will have the option of buying your negatives—most photographers require you to wait several years so that they can continue to sell the proofs if you want pictures made. Make sure that you understand all elements of the "package." Ask questions about the number and size of proofs you'll receive; the cost of additional prints and enlargements; and the costs of special techniques, such as hand-coloring, Polaroid transfers, and art borders. If you'd like to e-mail your pictures, or post them on the Internet, ask your photographer if she can provide you with pictures on disk or shoot parts of your wedding with a digital camera or if your proofs will appear on the photographer's Web site.

ENGAGEMENT PHOTOGRAPHS

If you book your photographer early, it's a great idea to have her shoot your engagement picture as well as your wedding day. No longer just a head shot of the bride, engagement pictures may now include the groom. Having a professional picture of the two of you not in wedding-day clothes is a great option, and, because they are not wedding-day shots, engagement pictures tend to "date" less than wedding portraits. If you do plan to have your engagement announced in the paper, be sure to find out the picture requirements and let your photographer know what they are. (See chapter 1 for more information on newspaper announcements.)

BRIDAL PORTRAITS

If you wish to have an heirloom portrait, display your portrait at the reception, or announce your wedding in the newspaper, you will need to have a bridal portrait. A bridal portrait can be just as fun or as formal (or both) as you like—taken in a studio, or out of doors, or both. A portrait is usually taken about two months prior to the wedding, so your dress, veil, and accessories must be ready well in advance. Many photographers offer a hair and makeup specialist for your bridal portrait, or they will let you bring your own. If you can afford it, this is a terrific option for your wedding day as well. Remember that if you don't absolutely love the way your hair and makeup looks, don't go ahead with the shoot. Let your photographer know you're not happy and either attempt to fix the problem or schedule the shoot for another day because, if you don't love the way you look, you're not going to love your portrait. Even if you don't want to go to the expense of having a bouquet professionally made for your portrait, buy some fresh flowers (ones that really reflect your personality) to hold. The idea that plastic or silk flowers will look real in a photograph is laughable. If you don't mind the groom's seeing you in your dress prior to the wedding, he can certainly appear in a portrait with you. Like you, he must be dressed exactly as he will be on the wedding day from tie to shoes to cufflinks. Again, go to the trouble of acquiring a real boutonniere. A wedding portrait is not a requirement; out of the many pictures you'll have taken on your wedding day you'll surely have one of you alone, albeit not a formal portrait.

> ### *Wedding Day Reflections*
>
>
>
> T he back of my dress was really beautiful, but incredibly, there isn't one picture of it before the skirt was bustled. I really regret not having told the photographer that I specifically wanted a shot of it.
>
> —Diana

PRE-CEREMONY PHOTOGRAPHS

Most photographers, in an effort to spare you endless post-ceremony photo shoots, will take pictures of you and your family prior to the ceremony. If you don't mind seeing the groom before the ceremony, the photographer can take all the posed shots. If, however, you don't want to see the groom until you walk down the aisle, your photographer will shoot you separately. Most photographers will ask you to give them a "must have" list of shots that are important to you. Take the time to think carefully about this and return a list, but don't make it too long or try to include every single possible shot. Ask your parents and future in-laws for their "must haves"—the photographer can't be expected to know that all your grandmother wants is a picture of her and the groom. Remember that it's better to have too many posed shots than too few—you can never go back if anything has been missed. Generally, "must haves" include:

- The bride

- The groom

- The bride and groom

- The bride and her maid/matron of honor

- The groom and his best man

- The bride with all her attendants

- The groom with all his attendants

- The bride and groom with all their attendants

- The bride with her parents (separately and together)

- The groom with his parents (separately and together)

- The bride and her family (aunts, uncles, etc.)

- The groom and his family (aunts, uncles, etc.)

- The bride and groom and their families

- The bride and her grandparents

- The groom and his grandparents

- The bride and her best friends (if they're not all in the wedding party)

- The groom and his best friends (if they're not all in the wedding party)

- The bride and her siblings (if they're not in the wedding party)

- The groom and his siblings (if they're not in the wedding party)

Check with your ceremony site or officiant to see what sort of photography is allowed during the ceremony and where your photographer can set up. If your photographer is unfamiliar with your site and its lighting, you may wish to schedule an appointment to meet her at the site, or a least give her enough time the day of the wedding to familiarize herself with her surroundings.

POST-CEREMONY PHOTOGRAPHS

At your rehearsal, be sure to explain to your attendants approximately how long your post-ceremony photographs will take. It is essential, especially if your ceremony and reception are held at the same location, that everyone stay together immediately after the ceremony. Tracking down groomsmen who've posted themselves in line at the bar can be exceptionally time-consuming and exasperating. Remember, the sooner you finish the pictures, the sooner you can join the reception. Keep in mind that, unless your family and wedding party are very small, you'll be involved in post-wedding pictures for thirty minutes to an hour.

RECEPTION PHOTOGRAPHY

"Must haves" for the reception include:

- The bride and groom's arrival

- The receiving line

Who Pays for Parents' Albums?

❧

My husband and I have just received the proofs from our wedding, which are wonderful. The photography package we chose included one album with 100 images (for my husband and me) and one parent's album with 50 images (for my mom and dad). Additional albums are $500 each. My parents have already paid for the photography, and this is the problem: My husband's parents have asked when they'll be getting their album. Well, frankly, they haven't ordered or paid for one, but, for some reason, they don't realize that it's not included in what my parents have bought. I hate to sound stingy, but my parents paid for the entire wedding, and I know they're not going to be happy if I tell them they need to spend another $500. How do I break it to my in-laws? They've also said that they want a copy of my bridal portrait, which cost $1,500 and I think is around $50 for a print. How do I ask them for that money?

- The bride and groom's first dance

- The bride and her father's dance

- The best man's toast

For some reason they don't realize that their album is not included in what your parents have already paid for? I wonder why that could be? Is it because you never told them? Your parents are not in any way obligated to buy an album for your in-laws; it's a lovely gesture if they're willing, but certainly not a requirement. It is your obligation, however, to circulate those wonderful proofs. You must either mail them (insured) to your in-laws, or if they live close by, deliver them to their house or ask them over to yours to peruse them. You should ask your photographer for an order form and price list, and be sure to give this to your in-laws along with the proofs. If they return the proofs with the order form filled out, but with no check, you have no choice but to tell them that their album has not been paid for. They then have the option of shelling out $500 or simply saying, "Oh, well, we just want the one of all of us together" and paying for only the print. As far as the bridal portrait goes, I hope you're not planning to figure any of the $1,500 into the cost of sending your in-laws a $50 print. In any case, your photographer can help you here, just ask her to send your in-laws the print along with a bill. Of course, since your parents paid for the entire wedding, which, although not unheard of, is generous nonetheless, perhaps you and your husband, who have paid nothing for all these lovely photos, could part with the $50 and give your portrait to your in-laws as a present.

- The maid of honor toasting

- The groom toasting

- The bride toasting

- The bride and groom cutting the cake

- The bride and groom feeding each other the cake

- The garter toss

- The bouquet toss

- The bride and groom leaving the reception

CANDID PHOTOGRAPHS

If you'd like pictures of every guest (that is if your guest list is very small), let your photographer know, especially if you're going to use them as thank yous. Also let your photographer know if you'd like the pictures to be posed, or movement, or a combination of the two.

Guests and Photography

MANY couples choose to give disposable cameras to guests in order to capture candid and or/posed shots. Most photographers do not mind if this is the case, but their photography must take precedence over anyone else's. Many photographers include a clause in their contract that ensures that they are the only professional photographer shooting your wedding. Keep this in mind before asking your brother-in-law, who is a professional commercial photographer, to take pictures at your reception; your photographer will not tolerate his being in her way.

Why Choose Videography?

A video can capture all the parts of your wedding day, particularly the reception, that you miss. A well-made video is a treasure, for you, your parents, and future generations. The quality of video has really improved over the past few years due to technological advances in equipment.

A standard wedding video can include a great deal. Still photographs of the couples' childhood and their courtship are often included, as well as the entire wedding day—from the bride's getting ready to the ceremony and reception, including interviews with guests and family. Music is often added along with various special effects. Average edited videos are about an hour in length. Resist the urge to request a longer video, even at an hour you'll still be fast-forwarding.

Hiring a Videographer

LIKE the photographer, look for a videographer with whom you really click. In fact, your photographer is probably your best source for videographer recommendations. When you meet a videographer for the first time, rely on your instincts—if you feel she's going to be intrusive or pushy, you're probably right. Ask to see several wedding videos and remember when you watch them that you're looking for the quality of the video not the style of the wedding, which reflects the bride and groom's tastes, not the videographer's. In other words, the fact that the bridesmaid's dresses are the ugliest you've ever seen should not mar your overall opinion of the videographer's work. The videos should be clear and well lit, not dark or fuzzy. Cuts from one shot to another should be seamless, not choppy, and the sound quality should be absolutely clear. You should ask the videographer what sort of equipment she'll be using; a digital format produces the best video and requires little light. Older equipment, such as a Betacam, requires a great deal of light and can be highly intrusive. You should ask the videographer what sort of involvement, if any, you will have in editing the footage, and how soon after the wedding you will be able to view it. Many videographers will charge you a set rate to shoot the video and an additional cost depending on the level of editing and special effects that you choose. You should also ask if you are able to keep the original footage and if not, then for how long does the videographer keep it (in case you need extra copies or if yours is damaged). Ask how the raw footage will be edited; nonlinear (digital) editing creates a better quality than linear (tape to tape). Be specific about what you do and don't want the videographer to capture. If, for instance, you don't want guest interviews or footage of your getting ready, be sure to let her know this in advance. As with photography, let your videographer know of any "must have" moments you'd like captured. Both she and the photographer should be provided with a timeline of your reception as well as a ceremony program so they'll know what to expect and when. Be sure to clear videography with your ceremony site prior to shopping for videographers. Many sites have very strict rules concerning videography and lighting (many will not allow lights), so be certain that your videographer is familiar with the site, its lighting, and its rules. In order for your vows to be heard clearly on the tape, you may well need to employ a microphone for the ceremony. If you are having an outdoor ceremony in a location where power does not exist, you should practice saying your vows loudly and clearly well before the big day.

Wedding Day Reflections

I had requested the Etta James classic "At Last" for my first dance; unfortunately, the DJ played another artist's version of the song. My videographer knew that I was really disappointed about the mix-up, and when I received the video, she had dubbed over the song with the Etta James version. Perfect!

—Kelley

The Contract: Get It in Writing

As with other wedding vendors, don't hand over any money to your photographer or videographer without having first signed a contract. A good contract will include the following elements from either a photographer or videographer:

Date and time of the ceremony and reception

Name of the person who will shoot the wedding and the assistant if applicable

Location(s) at which you'd like the photographer/videographer to shoot

Photographer's/videographer's start and estimated finish times

Number of proofs you'll receive and the number of rolls of film that will be shot

Package details such as size of prints, number of albums, etc.

Cost of additional videos

Estimated length of the finished video

Estimated delivery time of proofs/video

Total cost

Deposit requirement

Overtime cost

Cancellation and refund policy

Timeless Traditions

If you love the look of your parents' or even grandparents' wedding movie, consider hiring a videographer who shoots with a Super-8 camera and black and white film (which is different than video—think old-fashioned projector). The look is very beautiful, with great contrast between light and dark, a very grainy texture, and lends itself to an artistically shot video. A well-edited black and white Super-8 film, dubbed with appropriate music, can be truly stunning.

Manners and Your Photographer/Videographer

YOUR photographer/videographer should be offered food and drink at your reception, to exclude them from the guest count is in very poor taste. Photographers/videographers, like any other wedding professional, do not drink alcohol at the reception. Photographers/videographers should be dressed professionally, although they needn't match the guests' formality if there are tuxedos and ball gowns involved. Photographers/videographers should endeavor to be as unobtrusive as possible and refrain from taking pictures/footage of anyone that later prove to be embarrassing. Photographers should be told in advance if you are planning to have a videographer at your wedding, and, if photographs are your priority, you should let your videographer know so that her filming does not intrude on the photographer's picture taking.

Film-Damage Insurance

IT is now possible to purchase insurance that will cover your photography in case the film is lost or damaged. While nothing can replace your reception shots, insurance will cover the cost of getting your wedding party back together for a reshoot.

Etiquette for Friends and Guests

FRIENDS and guests should realize that photography is expensive and should not attempt to preorder shots of themselves. That goes for the wedding party, too. Relatives should rest assured that they'll receive a picture of themselves along with the bride and groom, but should certainly not expect an album filled with images. You can certainly

Dos & Don'ts

🌿

Do choose a photographer whose style you love.

Do book your photographer well ahead of time.

Do choose a photographer whose personality you enjoy.

Do find out what parents' expectations of your wedding photography are.

Do find out what families want prior to ordering wedding packages.

Do include the groom in your engagement portrait.

Do let your photographer know if you're not happy with your hair or makeup *before* the shoot begins.

Do keep your "must haves" list as short as possible.

Do check with your ceremony site to find out restrictions on photography/ videography.

Do feed your videographer/photographer.

Do hire a videographer who uses state-of-the-art equipment.

Do let your photographer know if you're hiring a videographer.

Do get a contract in writing.

Don't skimp on hiring a photographer's assistant if one has been recommended.

Don't feel obligated to have a formal wedding portrait.

ask the bride what the cost of such an album would be and ask her to order one (after she's received your check) on your behalf. Friends who see the engagement and/or wedding-portrait pictures prior to the event should only make complimentary remarks on how wonderful the bride and or groom look in the photographs, unless the quality of the picture taking itself is obviously poor. Those who see the wedding portrait ahead of time kindly refrain from telling anyone, especially the groom, what the dress looks like.

12

A NIGHT ON THE TOWN

Etiquette and the Bachelor(ette) Party

Tʜᴇ ʙᴀᴄʜᴇʟᴏʀ ᴘᴀʀᴛʏ is an old tradition, once relegated to only the groom and his friends; it has now been widely adopted by the bride and hers. The idea that once couples are married they can no longer socialize with single friends is an outdated idea, although one which underscores the origins of this tradition. So what is the proper way to celebrate the shift from single life to married? This chapter will help you to breath new life into the bachelor(ette) party, as well as help answer questions such as "Should we have the bachelor party right before the wedding, when everyone is in town?" and "Who pays for the party and who should send the invitations?" Since the ladies are now diving headlong into the practice of bachelorette parties, this chapter will help them steer clear of the pitfalls that have long plagued the gentlemen's corresponding celebration. Please note that in this chapter the words "bachelor" and "bachelorette" are used interchangeably.

Planning the Party

WHEN TO HOLD THE PARTY

Gone are the days when the rehearsal dinner was nonexistent and the bachelor party was held the night prior to the wedding. Never a good idea, the fading of this tradition is welcome. It is preferable to hold the bachelor party the weekend prior to the wedding, or even before that. If many of the wedding party live out of town, it is considerate to hold the bachelor party long before the wedding so that groomsmen and bridesmaids do not have to make two trips in a row, or even in the same month.

Single Sex or Coed?

The idea that the bride's and groom's attendants must be all the same sex is old-fashioned and outdated. There is no reason, therefore, that if the bride has a best man or a groomsman he should be excluded from her bachelorette party; the same goes for the groom if he has a maid of honor or a bridesmaid. If the bride and groom have many friends of both sexes in common, there is no reason to split them according to sex and have two parties. No rule exists which dictates that the bride and groom must have separate bachelor parties. One party for both the bride and groom, provided they are in agreement with the concept, is perfectly correct. Keep in mind though, that if the bachelor party is to be coed, the activities should be acceptable to both sexes. Trips to a salon for a makeover and manicure or an evening at a "gentlemen's" club are not likely to appeal to both men and women.

INCLUDING SPOUSES

It is quite logical to include spouses at a coed bachelor party but not logical if the party is otherwise single sex. Married bridesmaids, groomsmen, and other bachelor-party guests attending single-sex parties should keep in mind that behavior fitting a bachelor is only marginally appropriate for the bride or groom and inappropriate for themselves.

WHO PAYS?

Although tradition once dictated that the groom pay for the bachelor dinner, it is more usual these days to see the best man and/or groomsmen pitch in and pay for the groom, then in turn each pay for themselves. The same applies to the ladies. Unless the party is going to cost a set amount, which can be prepaid, an estimate of funds may be collected for the evening and put into one person's account (generally the best man's or maid of honor's). This is a great deal simpler than having to divide the check among many individuals. If you do decide to go with separate checks in the interest of fairness, it is important that the bride/groom's share be divided equally among the others attending.

WHO IS INVITED?

All members of the wedding party (with the obvious exception of flower girls and ring bearers if the entertainment is to be adult) should be invited and endeavor to attend the bachelorette party. If either the bride's or groom's parent(s) are members of the wedding party, they should also attend the bachelor party. Close friends who have not been included in the wedding party may certainly be invited to the bachelorette party.

Wedding Day Reflections

My best man didn't plan anything for a bachelor party, and I really didn't think it was a big deal. Anyway, we spent some of the night before my wedding making up for it I guess, by going to one of those wings-and-beer places where all the girls wear tight tank tops. It just wasn't that much fun. In retrospect, I wish I'd hinted that I wanted to do something way before the wedding.

—James

The Bride and the Bachelor Party

❧

My fiancé and I are in the midst of planning our wedding and have already had disagreements about several things, mainly, his groomsmen. His best man and three groomsmen are all college fraternity brothers, and frankly, behave like frat boys. I really don't think it's appropriate in this day and age for them to throw my fiancé that whole "stripper nightclub" kind of bachelor party, but my fiancé insists he has no control over it and if I want to do anything about it, I should call the best man. Secondly, I refuse to do that whole "garter" thing, which I think is very tacky. My fiancé wants me to plan the bouquet toss so that my maid of honor will catch it, while he arranges the garter thing so that the best man will do the same etc. etc. I'm also afraid of what they'll do to my car, which is the one we'll be using to leave the reception.

How do I exercise control over five grown men?" I presume, is your question. Let us address your first concern, the bachelor party. Your fiancé does have some say in the situation, unless of course, the party is planned completely as a surprise, with no care given to what he may or may not enjoy. Your calling the best man and making recommendations is not appropriate and will only make you look like a shrew. If your fiancé has the opportunity to express his opinion about the entertainment, care must be taken not to make you out to be the wet blanket. He *must be prepared to say, "You know, I'd really rather have dinner at the new martini/cigar club than a strip club" rather than "I'd love to go, but the ball-and-chain won't go for it."*

A bride's throwing tantrums and feigning horror over bachelor parties isn't really appropriate "in this day and age" either. Since you dislike the fact that these men "behave like frat boys" I assume you've chosen to marry the only one in the bunch prepared to behave like a mature gentleman. Therefore, I'm sure you can rest assured that your fiancé will never participate in any activity likely to cause you distress. If you cannot, the bachelor party is the very least of your problems.

As far as the "garter" thing goes, I tend to agree that the whole ritual is rarely accomplished in good taste. Orchestrated bouquet throwing, concluding with the maid of honor's stepping on heads in order to complete the catch, is also "tacky." I offer a simple solution to your car problem. Don't drive it. Instead, hire a chauffeured car or limousine. The chauffeur will no doubt stand guard and the groomsmen will find themselves quite limited as to what they may or may not do to a rented automobile.

As you take precautions against frat-boy antics, take heed of the following urban legend: The morning after their wedding, a bride and groom were discussing the beauty of their honeymoon accommodations, and how surprised and relived they were not to have been subjected to his groomsmen's fraternity-style pranks. The groom then phoned room service, requesting "Breakfast for two." At that point, from beneath the bed, the best man spoke up, "Make that six."

GIFTS

An invitation to a bachelorette party does not carry with it the obligation of a gift. Any attempt to turn a bachelorette party into a wedding shower is prohibited. Very often gifts for the wedding party are distributed at the bachelor party—although if it's held several months prior to the wedding, it's perfectly fine to wait to give presents until the bridesmaid's luncheon or rehearsal dinner.

INVITATIONS

Invitations to a bachelor party should correspond to the formality of the event. If there is to be a sit-down dinner at a restaurant or country club, written invitations should be issued, generally by the best man or maid of honor. If the evening is to consist of barhopping, a telephone call or e-mail may suffice. If a trip has been planned (to the beach, camping or fishing, etc.) details outlining cost, maps, meeting times, carpooling, and so forth may be mailed, telephoned, or e-mailed.

TRANSPORTATION

Although most definitely not a requirement, drinking is certainly a tradition of the bachelor party. If there is to be any drinking planned for the evening, safe transportation is a must and should be arranged long beforehand. Whether this means that everyone should be prepared to have enough cash on them for a taxi or that a chauffeured limo or car is hired ahead of time, there is absolutely no excuse whatsoever for drinking and driving. Even if a non-drinker in your crowd offers to be designated driver, think twice before taking her up on it. Would you want to be the sober one responsible for a groom and six other groomsmen at four in the morning?

Party Themes

FOR THE GENTLEMEN

The ubiquitous "drinking and strip club" bachelor parties of old, although still done, are rather out of fashion. Far more modern is a gathering at a restaurant for a good dinner, followed, perhaps by a visit to a cigar or martini bar. Also popular are weekend-away bachelor parties, particularly for outdoor types. No doubt a weekend spent fishing and/or camping is likely to prove more memorable (literally) than an evening spent applying dollar bills, with varying degrees of accuracy, to a complete stranger's undergarments.

FOR THE LADIES

It is unfortunate, now that gentlemen are phasing out the strip club/drunken debauchery bachelor party, that ladies appear to be under the impression that they have been passed the torch. The idea of equality does not mean that ladies should pick up the same bad habits they have encouraged gentlemen to shed. If drinking layered shots at a strip club is the most meaningful way one can imagine to spend time with one's closest girlfriends, then so be it—there are, however, alternatives. As with the gentlemen, weekend getaways are popular, whether camping, hiking, fishing, or sunning on the beach. A group visit to a spa or salon followed by an evening out to a good restaurant is also a more civilized choice than paying perfectly good money to see some man's oily chest, which one could presumably view at the beach for free.

Wedding Day Reflections

I didn't have a bachelorette party per se, but two days before my wedding, my mom, my future mother-in-law, my two brides-maids, my brother's girlfriend, and I went out to dinner at a wonderful restaurant. After the moms left, we all shared a bottle of champagne and toasted one another. It was really wonderful, plus I was home by ten and didn't have a hangover the next day.

—Diana

The Bachelorette Party and Good Taste

🌿

I have a very close friend who recently asked me to be a brides-maid at her wedding. Her sister is maid of honor and she is go-ing to organize a bachelorette party. We were all out on the town a few weeks ago, and at the same bar was a bachelorette party. Good grief! The bride was dressed up in a veil, to which someone (I assume her bridesmaids) had affixed a number of condoms. In her hand was a pink and very lifelike—well, you get the picture. They sat up at the bar drinking (I won't say the name of it) a drink topped with whipped cream that one is sup-posed to drink as a shot—with no hands touching the glass. I was enormously embarrassed for them. My friend's sister, who is six years younger than the rest of us, thought all of this seemed like great fun, and the next day told me that she's planning to orchestrate a similar shindig for her sister's bachelorette party. I'm appalled—I really don't want to be part of such a ridiculous scene. Since I'm not the maid of honor, what say, if any, do I have in organizing this ritual? When we were out, by the way, the party we witnessed also embarrassed my friend, the bride.

Equality between the sexes has come a long way. I am a strong advocate of equal opportunity, equal pay for equal work, paternity leave for fathers, diaper-changing stations in the men's room, and the like. I am not, however, an advocate of ladies adopting (or even embellishing) bad habits that were once the sole terrain of gentlemen. I do not object to the bride's wearing a veil to signify her upcoming nuptials, however, one wonders what the application of condoms could possibly signify. The idea that the bride should have some handy for a last fling is in exceptionally poor taste. The addition of the "pink and very lifelike" item is also puzzling and one wonders how many bars would allow gentlemen to belly up carrying a corresponding "pink and very lifelike" part of the female anatomy. With that said, the point here is that your friend the bride was embarrassed for the members of the bachelorette party, and therefore you may intervene hastily, and tactfully. I suggest you get together with her sister and the other bridesmaids in order to hash out a plan for the party. To this meeting, I suggest you bring, after first soliciting it from the bride, a list of her top five activities for a bachelorette party. Since the condom sporting barhop will be omitted from the list, it may be difficult for the maid of honor to pitch the idea as one the bride will enjoy. Keep in mind, however, that no matter how refined an activity you decide on, the maid of honor may still show up with props. It is up to the bride, not you, to good-naturedly refuse them.

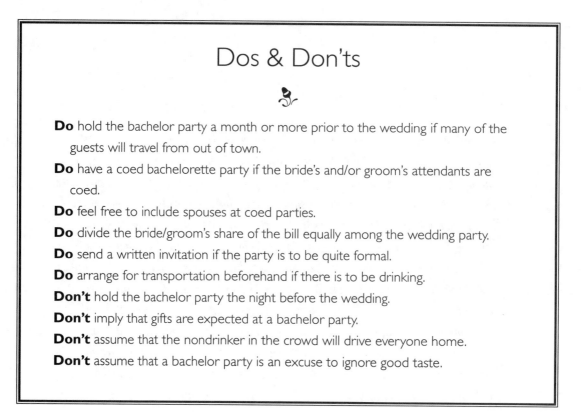

Dos & Don'ts

❦

Do hold the bachelor party a month or more prior to the wedding if many of the guests will travel from out of town.

Do have a coed bachelorette party if the bride's and/or groom's attendants are coed.

Do feel free to include spouses at coed parties.

Do divide the bride/groom's share of the bill equally among the wedding party.

Do send a written invitation if the party is to be quite formal.

Do arrange for transportation beforehand if there is to be drinking.

Don't hold the bachelor party the night before the wedding.

Don't imply that gifts are expected at a bachelor party.

Don't assume that the nondrinker in the crowd will drive everyone home.

Don't assume that a bachelor party is an excuse to ignore good taste.

Etiquette for Friends and Guests

As with all invitations, guests should RSVP as quickly as possible, then stick with their affirmative reply. The idea that, because one might be paying for one's own refreshments, one may back out of a "yes" reply the morning of the party because of some fluctuation in finances is rude. If transportation is organized for all guests everyone should take advantage of the same. If at the beginning of the evening any guest feels better served by driving himself, but at the end of the evening is impaired to do so he should be prepared to heed the encouragement to "Just get in the limo." Guests should not encourage the party to move to another venue because "this place is dead," nor should they encourage activities not on the evening's agenda without a consensus of opinion by the rest of the party and the guest of honor. Friends and guests should not reflect morosely to the bride or groom that "I guess this'll be the last time we'll get to do this now you're getting married." Such sentiments are dreary and old-fashioned. Friends should, if necessary, monitor the behavior of the guest of honor and *never, ever* encourage them to engage in any activity that would prove difficult, if not impossible, to explain to their fiancée or fiancé.

PRACTICE MAKES PERFECT

ETIQUETTE AND THE REHEARSAL

Rehearsing the wedding ceremony is absolutely essential with the possible exception of small civil ceremonies that take place at a courthouse or other location. For all other weddings, even if you have only two attendants, it is prudent to practice the recessional and processional to the appropriate music and have a brief, although not necessarily complete, rundown of the entire ceremony, particularly readings and solos. This chapter will discuss exactly what is and what is not necessary to rehearse, who should and who should not be present, and the proper behavior for all those who attend. The rehearsal dinner, once an intimate affair consisting of only the wedding party and close family, has now become a larger event, sometimes even competing with the wedding for grandeur. This chapter gives you rehearsal dinner dos and don'ts and covers such essential questions as "Who hosts?," "What is the proper invitation wording?," and "Whom do we include?"

Organizing the Rehearsal

WHO SHOULD ATTEND THE CEREMONY REHEARSAL?

Whoever is to escort the bride, the parents of the bride and groom, plus all of the wedding party, including ushers, guest-book and program attendants, and all readers or soloists—in other words, anyone who will participate in the ceremony in any way should absolutely attend the rehearsal. When friends and family are asked to participate in the ceremony they should be immediately informed of their obligation to attend the rehearsal prior to their responding to the request. A stand-in must be arranged for any member of the wedding party who is unable to attend the rehearsal. Grandparents and very close family, if they are not members of the wedding party, may also attend. Parents of flower girls and ring bearers should also attend.

WHO SHOULD NOT ATTEND THE CEREMONY REHEARSAL?

Distant family, dates and spouses of members of the wedding party, and anyone else with no role in the wedding should not attend the rehearsal, even if they "don't want to sit around the hotel." Enough time should be allowed between the end of the rehearsal and the beginning of the rehearsal dinner to allow those involved in the rehearsal to either drive home or to the hotel to pick up their family members and/or dates. Conversely, spouses/dates may certainly deliver participants to the rehearsal, then pick them up

---

Wedding Day Reflections

Probably the biggest mistake I made was going out with the wedding party after the rehearsal dinner. We closed down a local bar. The next morning I had to pick up my cousins at the airport at 10:00 A.M., and I just felt lousy. The wedding wasn't until 5:00 P.M., but still I didn't have time for a nap.

—Winston

upon its conclusion. If this is utterly impossible, those not involved in the rehearsal but who attend the same should sit quietly in any pew and refrain from making a nuisance of themselves.

WHAT TIME TO REHEARSE?

In order to allow in-town guests a full day's work, and out-of-town guests a full day's travel, weekday rehearsals are ideally held in the late afternoon, around four or five o'clock is customary. If your wedding party consists of all in-towners who are largely unemployed or generally at leisure, you may certainly plan your rehearsal for earlier in the day. Just make sure there is a consensus. No one wants to call in sick at an hourly-wage/no-paid-vacation job in order to attend your rehearsal.

HIRING A WEDDING DIRECTOR

Unless your house of worship provides its own wedding director, it is essential to employ one for your rehearsal and ceremony. (Even if your wedding consultant also directs weddings, be sure to check with your house of worship. Many do not allow outside directors.) Enlisting family members to direct your wedding is not wise, even if they direct weddings professionally. Family members, unlike strictly professional wedding planners, are likely to take the fact that your cousin Emily— who is your bridesmaid and whose daughter is the flower girl—arrived twenty minutes late to the rehearsal as an affront to the whole family. Professional directors, on the other hand, will simply replace tardy principals with stand-ins and move on. Family members also will be caught up in the inevitable socializing surrounding a wedding. It is difficult for your aunt to direct a ceremony when she's deep in conversation with her sister-in-law, whom she "hasn't seen for ages."

MEETING WITH A WEDDING DIRECTOR

If your wedding planner will not also act as your director, endeavor to hire a director as soon as possible after your engagement. Ask your church for recommendations and be sure to request references from any candidate. You should meet at least once prior to the rehearsal in order to go over the order of your processional and recessional (see chapter 8 for more information), the number of readings and solos, and to review your music choices and ceremony in general. As soon as your wedding program goes to print, provide the proof to your wedding director. She should use this as a basis for creating an accurate timeline and a list of instructions to provide to you and your wedding party at the rehearsal.

> ### Timeless Traditions
>
>
>
> It used to be considered bad luck for the bride to participate in her own wedding rehearsal; usually she chose a stand-in and simply watched from the sidelines. This practice is no longer considered practical and most brides are eager to rehearse until practice makes perfect.

THE OFFICIANT

While it is not absolutely positively necessary for your officiant to attend your rehearsal, she should make every endeavor to do so. If she is unable to attend, enlist someone to act in her stead, which means, of course, that the stand-in should have the entire copy of the ceremony ahead of time. Your wedding director should be able to fill the officiant's shoes if necessary.

MUSICIANS

It is unwise to conduct a rehearsal without the musicians you've hired for your ceremony. Music provides many of your cues, and without it, you'll be lost. The wedding party's timeline and instructions for the ceremony should be given to all musicians and your musical director, if applicable, along with a copy of the program prior to the rehearsal if possible.

Rehearsing the Wedding

NAME TAGS OR T-SHIRTS

Name tags or T-shirts embellished with the titles "Maid of Honor," "Best Man," and so on are a good idea at the rehearsal, especially if your wedding party is large. Name tags are especially helpful to wedding directors, who will, for example, have a list of names indicating the lineup of bridesmaids, but unlike you, will have absolutely no idea which name belongs to which face. Name tags must be removed prior to the rehearsal dinner, as should T-shirts. This should not be construed as a way to kick off the evening's activities with a bang; T-shirts should be replaced (in private) by whatever the dinner's dress code dictates.

LOGISTICS

The bride should inform all those who are to participate in the rehearsal to arrive at least fifteen minutes prior to the starting time. She does not, for obvious reasons, tell anyone that the given time is "a few minutes early, we don't really have to be there 'til five." Keep in mind that many rehearsals take place on a Friday, just around rush hour, so do take traffic into account when giving people estimated travel times. Those participating or attending the rehearsal arrive sober and do not turn up, even if the rehearsal takes place in a meadow, holding a beer. The maid of honor is responsible for delivering the bride on time; the best man is responsible for delivering the groom; other adults are responsible for themselves. Once assembled at the ceremony site, those not participating in the ceremony should immediately sit

> ### Timeless Traditions
>
> It is traditional for all the ribbons from the bridal shower to be made into a bouquet for the bride to use as a stand-in during the rehearsal. It's a good idea to make one for the maid/matron of honor too so that she can practice taking the bride's and holding both.

down. A wedding rehearsal is not a sort of pre-cocktail-hour party during which friends and family take the opportunity to catch up. Whether the ceremony takes place in a cathedral or a living room, the space should be treated with the reverence that befits a wedding. Those involved in the wedding should listen carefully to the wedding director and refrain from disappearing from the lineup to go and say "hey" to pals not participating. Once the group is assembled, the processional should be rehearsed, as well as readings, solos, and however much of the ceremony the bride and groom wish to practice. (Some refrain from saying the entirety of their vows; those that have written their own vows in secret as a surprise do not practice them at all.) The handoff of the bouquet should be practiced, as should the lifting of the blusher (part of the veil that covers the face) although the bride need not wear it, as well as the giving of the rings and any other intrinsic part of the ceremony. If the bride's dress has a very long train, she should tie a length of fabric at her waist so that the maid of honor can practice arranging it. The recessional should also be practiced. If groomsmen are to return to escort mothers and grandmothers or to release pews, this should be practiced also. If the group is well-organized, moderately lucid, and on time, a run-through of the ceremony, twice performed, should be sufficient.

BRIDES AND GROOMS AND THE REHEARSAL

If the bride and groom have given their director all the specifics necessary to orchestrate a successful rehearsal, no more input should be necessary. The bride should resist the urge to assist in directing her friends and family members. Remember that on the big day you'll be tucked away in a room until the processional. Giving direction during the rehearsal confuses those participating (and generally gets on the director's nerves). Brides and grooms should also realize that the rehearsal and rehearsal dinner will not afford you quality time with each other. Especially when many friends and family members have traveled far, the emphasis will likely be on their socializing with the two of you, rather than the two of you socializing with each other. Instead of getting huffy because it seems as if your future spouse is ignoring you, brides and grooms should use this tiny window of opportunity to take a little break from each other before the big day.

The Rehearsal Dinner

THE rehearsal dinner is generally held right after the rehearsal in a location convenient to both the ceremony site and out-of-town guests' hotel rooms. For the sake of surprise, the rehearsal dinner is not usually held at the same site as the reception. Those who are hosting the rehearsal dinner, particularly if they happen to be the groom's parents, should take extreme care not to, even inadvertently, outdo the wedding reception. This means that the wedding menu and type of reception should be chosen prior to planning the rehearsal-dinner menu and format (see chapter 9 for wedding reception styles and menus). An intimate sit-down dinner for 20 may certainly precede a buffet-style wedding reception for 200, but a black-tie, sit-down, filet mignon and lobster rehearsal dinner for 125 would be in poor taste if it is to be followed by a casual afternoon tea-sandwich wedding reception.

WHO HOSTS?

Generally the groom's parents host the rehearsal dinner, although this is not a hard and fast rule. Anyone or any combination of people may host the dinner, even the bride and groom themselves.

Name Tags at the Rehearsal Dinner

❧

My mother, my fiancée, and I are having quite a heated debate over name tags. My parents are, of course, hosting the rehearsal dinner. There will be about sixty guests for a sit-down dinner—the wedding party, both sets of parents, the minister, and pretty much everyone who's coming in from out of town the Friday prior to the wedding will be attending. With so many people who've never met, I think it would be great to give people name tags at the dinner. My mom agrees with me—like me, she attends many events where name tags are par for the course. My fiancée, on the other hand, objects strongly. Who is right?

In the old days a rehearsal dinner was an intimate event made up of those who had actually participated in the wedding rehearsal. Now, unfortunately, hosts feel compelled to include every guest who may be traveling the day before or anyone else who, heaven forbid, should find themselves with "nothing to do" the evening prior to a wedding. Dining at one's hotel, mingling with the other out-of-town guests staying there, and getting a good night's sleep appear to no longer appeal to today's wedding guest. The rehearsal dinner is not an ancient custom and is by no means obligatory, but, in these days of increasingly elaborate weddings,

WHO PAYS?

Generally the hosts pay all or part of the bill. If the bride and/or groom pay for the entire thing but wish for their parents only to be listed on the invitation, that is their choice. Jockeying for a higher ranking on the invitation by those paying more of the bill than others is considered a lack of good taste.

it often turns out to be as grand as the reception itself, with almost as many guests. You and your parents may choose to give any kind of rehearsal dinner you wish, but you may not confuse it with a corporate affair. Name tags are a grand idea at fundraisers, office events, or corporate gatherings. The leftover name tags reveal an accurate overall head count, plus identify the no-shows. Since corporate events have nothing to do with genuine social life, it is quite all right to read "John Smith, Vice President, Human Resources, Right Corp." on someone's upper torso. What would you have your name tags read? "Betty Ann Smith, college friend of the bride, Boise, Idaho" or "John Smith, uncle of the bride"? Will you be wearing a name tag? Your parents? The bride and her parents? Your fiancée is right, there should be no such thing as a name tag at a social event. "With so many people who've never met," your best bet may be to have a cocktail hour before a seated dinner, during which guests may approach others in a manner such as this: "Hello, I'm Margaret Smith. I'm the bride's sister and maid of honor. How nice to see you." To which the reply may be: "My pleasure. I'm Jake Adams. I'm the groom's cousin; I just flew in from New York." I don't doubt that about sixty guests can meet and mingle quite readily without such charming corporate helpmates as name tags, PowerPoint presentations, overhead projectors, podiums, and souvenir travel coffee mugs.

WHO SHOULD ATTEND?

The wedding party (without spouses/significant others if they are all local or with spouses/significant others if any are from out of town), the officiant, and immediate family members. Out-of-town guests, distant relatives, and close friends may or may not be included according to the hosts' wishes and budget.

INVITATIONS

Invitations should be congruent with the formality of the event; however, they should not exceed or even approach the degree of formality of the wedding invitations. If the affair is to be very casual, invitations may be issued by telephone or e-mail. The invitations should go out about five weeks prior to the wedding.

SEATING

Since a rehearsal dinner should be conducive to mingling, it's a good idea to start things off with a stand-up cocktail hour (whether alcohol is served or not) with butlered or buffet-style hors d'oeuvres. Assigned tables are as correct as assigned seating (see chapter 9 for more information about seating). Since a rehearsal dinner includes speeches and toasts, it is very important that everyone present have his own seat.

PHOTOGRAPHY

If your budget allows, it is wonderful to hire a professional photographer (preferably the one who will shoot your wedding) for the rehearsal dinner. Everyone is likely to be relaxed, which makes for great candid shots. This is also a great opportunity for the bride and groom to have pictures taken of them in something other than wedding attire. The absence of this attire often makes for pictures that "date" less than those taken on the actual wedding day. Disposable cameras placed on guest tables are also a nice idea, but when you take the film to be developed, be sure it's to a place that will refund your money even if the error in the picture is the fault of the photographer. You don't want to end up paying for an overabundance of bad pictures taken by amateurs. Be sure to tape cards on the cameras that read "Please leave the camera on your table at the end of the evening."

ENTERTAINMENT

Since a rehearsal dinner is not really a party per se, dance bands designed to "rock you 'til dawn" don't work especially well. In deference to speeches and toasts, music should be more background than anything. DJs (providing they are not chatty) are fine, as are pianists, string quartets, jazz bands, and the like. Since speeches and toasts provide much of the evening's entertainment, it's a good idea to have a microphone available for those making them. Podiums are for business presentations and Oscar acceptance speeches—they are not necessary at rehearsal dinners.

TOASTS

The first toast is generally given by the host, usually the groom's father. The groom's mother may also offer a toast or words of welcome. Friends and family members may make toasts as they wish, as may members of the wedding party, including the bride and groom. Toasts should be made during dinner only, should not drag on endlessly, and should never be risqué or embarrassing. The best man may toast if he likes, but this does not excuse him from making a (different) toast at the wedding.

Wedding Day Reflections

The most embarrassing part of the rehearsal dinner was the toasts my fiancé's fraternity brothers gave. They got up one after the other and went on and on about my fiancé's college escapades. I was mortified! I wish we'd cut off toasts after the four scheduled ones had been made.

—Stephanie

The Day Before the Wedding and Out-of-Town Guests

WHEN one expects many out-of-town guests to attend the wedding, it is wise to send out "save the date" cards (see chapter 5 for more information). Assuming that most guests will be staying at either of one or two hotels, it is gracious to acknowledge their presence. "Goodie bags" placed in hotel rooms are an excellent way to let guests know that you appreciate their traveling to attend your wedding. The bags need not be expensive: a personal note, bottled water, cookies, a "Things to Do" sheet, and directions to both the ceremony and the reception (very often the ones you may have sent with the invitation are still stuck on the fridge at home) are thoughtful and quite sufficient, although goodie bags may be as elaborate as your budget is able to withstand. If you have several events planned for guests during the weekend, or if you are providing transportation for guests, it's also a good idea to provide them with itineraries. For example:

Friday, June 21st

1:00 P.M.
Tee Time
Royal Pines Country Club
1800 Country Club Drive
6:30 P.M.
Cocktails and Rehearsal Dinner
Le Bistro
410 Bank Street

Saturday, June 22nd

Shuttle for Tour of Historic Savannah
Leaves at 11:00 A.M. from The Bay Street Inn
Returns to The Bay Street Inn at 3:00 P.M.
Shuttle from The Bay Street Inn to the Ceremony
Leaves at 6:30 P.M.
Shuttle from the Ceremony to the Reception
Leaves Immediately after the Ceremony

Shuttle Service from the Reception to The Bay Street Inn
Begins at 9:30 P.M.

Sunday, May 6th

11:00 A.M. Until 2:00 P.M.
Drop-In Brunch
at the home of
Mr. and Mrs. Harold James Phillips
1786 Sea Otter Drive

If prearranged activities require an accurate head count, "sign up" sheets should be included in the "save the date" cards. A map with the location of each activity, marked with a star, is essential. Provide the concierge at the hotel with extra itineraries and maps for those guests who misplace theirs.

OUT-OF-TOWN GUESTS AND ENTERTAINMENT

Hosts are not in any way obligated to entertain out-of-town guests nor are they obligated to include them at the rehearsal dinner. If many of your guests are from out of town, and are staying at the same hotel or at one of several in close proximity to each other, you may wish to treat them to cocktail hour on the evening prior to the wedding or during the evening after a daytime wedding. An invitation, placed in a goodie bag, might read:

Please enjoy cocktail hour
at
The Bay Street Inn
6700 Bay Street
On Friday, June 21st
from 6:00 P.M. until 7:30 P.M.
Susan and Harold Phillips

(continues on page 253)

Rehearsal Dinner Complications

❧

My son is getting married in six months; he lives in his fiancée's hometown about a half-hour away from us. Since everyone is fairly nearby, my husband and I would like to throw the rehearsal dinner here at our home. I would like to invite the bridal party (eight persons) and six guests who are coming from out of town that Friday. This brings the total to twenty-one including my husband and me, the minister, the bride's parents, and the bride and groom. I have heard, albeit secondhand, that the bride would rather the dinner be held at a restaurant in her hometown and wants the spouses of married groomsmen and bridesmaids (a total of six) to be invited as well. Since none of the bridal party is traveling from out of town, I didn't think I had to invite the spouses. What about the single bridesmaids and groomsmen? Will they want to bring dates when they find out that the married ones are bringing spouses? What, if any, concessions must I make to the bride? My husband and I are very happy for our son, but this whole rehearsal dinner is starting to dampen our enthusiasm.

The idea of throwing the rehearsal dinner at your home is charming— as hostess, you may choose whatever venue proves practical. Hearing things "second-

hand" from the bride is not a good sign, certainly at this stage of the game. I hope she is not asking your son to channel information to you, by the same token, I trust you are not asking the same of him. Unless the bride speaks directly to you, completely ignore her secondhand suggestions and ask the messenger to pipe down. If she actually tells you that she'd rather have the rehearsal dinner at a restaurant, reply with "You know, we hadn't even thought of that. That's a very interesting idea," then continue to do exactly as you please. If the bride becomes persistent and starts to spout recommendations prefaced with "You know, it's my wedding . . . "(The idea of "my wedding" is unfortunate, brides need to practice saying "our wedding" until it comes naturally), try a different approach. You might say: "Yes, I know how hard you and (insert groom's name) have worked to plan your wedding—you both must be exhausted! I just know you wouldn't want to plan this dinner on top of everything else, so just relax and let us take care of everything." Since none of the bridal party is traveling from out of town, no, you are not compelled to invite spouses. The idea that married people cannot spend one evening without each other's company is silly. However, if any of the wedding party were traveling from another city, I would certainly recommend that you include whomever has been invited to accompany them to the wedding, which of course would compel you to invite the "in-town" spouses as well. Out-of-town guests left to room service and mini bars while their better halves are wined and dined elsewhere have been known, during wedding receptions, to make loud, disparaging remarks about the color of the mother of the groom's shoes.

Dos & Don'ts

Do rehearse your ceremony, even if it's going to be simple and your wedding party is small.

Do make it clear that those not participating in the ceremony should not attend the wedding rehearsal.

Do schedule your rehearsal to allow in-towners a full day's work and out-of-towners a full day's travel.

Do hire a professional wedding director for your ceremony.

Do make sure that musicians are available to play for your rehearsal.

Do feel free to use name tags at your rehearsal, especially if your wedding party is large.

Do tell everyone who is attending that the rehearsal starts at least fifteen minutes prior to when it is actually scheduled.

Do pay attention to the wedding director.

Do cut off toasts after dinner has finished or if you feel the subject matter is deteriorating.

Do include "goodie bags" for out-of-town guests staying at hotels.

Do include itineraries and maps if you have activities planned for out-of-town guests.

Don't count on friends or family members to direct your wedding.

Don't try to direct the ceremony yourself.

Don't let the rehearsal dinner outdo the wedding reception.

Don't hire a loud dance band to perform at the rehearsal dinner.

Don't feel obligated to invite all out-of-town guests to your rehearsal dinner.

Don't stay out too late or drink too much at the rehearsal dinner.

(continued from page 249)

This is a delightful gesture, but if it is too extravagant for your budget, you might simply include the names of nearby restaurants on the "Things to Do" list in the goodie bag.

Etiquette for Friends and Guests

FRIENDS and guests should realize that they are attending a wedding only and that no one is under any obligation to entertain them in any other capacity, no matter how far they've traveled. Guests who have not been invited to the rehearsal dinner should find something else to do. Those who are intimidated by being in a strange town can sit in their hotel rooms, order room service, and watch cable without complaint. The rehearsal should be attended by the bride and groom, the wedding party, and close family only. There is no need for bridesmaids' boyfriends to be lolling about and getting in the way. If you absolutely positively have to attend the rehearsal without a role to play in the wedding, kindly sit down as soon as you get there and stay out of the way until everything is over. Guests RSVP to rehearsal dinner invitations with alacrity and do not call up the hostess and ask, "Can I bring a date?" No, you can't. Guests who wish to make toasts at the rehearsal dinner may do so, however, toasts must be premeditated, practiced at least once, and not reveal any information about the bride or groom previously unknown to each other or their parents, even if you think "It's not that big of a deal." Friends and guests who do not need to be awake until 5:00 P.M. the following day because the wedding isn't until 7:00 P.M. please note that this is not a luxury afforded to the bride or groom who should therefore be discouraged from drinking shots and staying out until 3:00 A.M.

14

HERE COMES THE BRIDE

ETIQUETTE FOR THE CEREMONY

ALL YOUR MONTHS of planning culminate here, at your wedding ceremony. Your religion and spiritual beliefs mandate the proper etiquette for your service, however, to ensure that your ceremony gets off to a proper start, a certain protocol should be followed. This chapter will help you make appropriate decisions regarding wedding party transportation, guest books, ceremony logistics, and receiving lines. It will also help you to decide what and what not to include in your wedding program, as well as help you to accomplish your pre- and post-wedding photography in a timely and organized fashion.

Wedding Party Transportation

IT is the bride's family's responsibility to pay for the wedding party's transportation to and from the ceremony and reception. A limousine is the traditional choice, but equally as correct, although perhaps not as photogenic, are passenger vans, town cars, and shuttle buses. If the weather and location are appropriate, a horse and carriage is a very romantic choice. No etiquette dictates who must travel with whom in what vehicle, although it is traditional, but not required, for the bride to travel with her father or whoever is to escort her.

The Guest Book

THE guest book need be nothing more than a bound volume of a few blank pages—good booksellers carry this sort of thing, which are often sold for use as journals or scrapbooks. It is not necessary to visit a "specialty" store and purchase a guest book with a quilted polyester satin cover, edged in lace with the words "Our Wedding" printed on it in florid script. The guest book basically acts as a sign-in sheet; after your wedding you can presumably review the book and pick out, by their lack of signature, those who RSVP'd "yes" but didn't show up. You can also use it to settle disputes—such as "Melanie Hall was *not* at our wedding!" "Oh yeah? Fifty bucks says she was . . ."—should they crop up years later. Guest books are by no means obligatory, or even necessary. In fact, very often couples are doing away with the guest book all together in favor of more personal writings. (See chapter 15 for more information on alternatives to guest books at the reception.) If you do choose to have your guests sign a guest book, it should be placed on a podium, table, or other level surface—

Wedding Day Reflections

At a wedding I attended, out-of-town guests were given detailed maps showing the route from the hotel to the ceremony, along with travel time. What we didn't know was that there was a huge concert on the evening of the wedding, and our route took us right by the coliseum where the band was playing. We were stuck for a half an hour. We were late to the ceremony (along with most of the other out-of-towners—the in-towners all knew alternate routes), which I hate. I wish the travel time on the map had been padded just a little bit—we might not have been late at all if it had.

—Mark

wherever is most convenient—either outside or inside the ceremony site. Although not a requirement, it's a good idea to ask someone to attend to the guest book and encourage all guests to sign. Unless the wedding is extremely large and guest book signings are creating a bottleneck into the ceremony, there is no reason why every guest cannot sign in. Accomplishing a complete sign-in at the ceremony circumvents having to bring the book to the reception site. The book should be accompanied by a pen of good quality, not, however, by one so great in value that its accidental placement into a guest's pocket will cause great consternation. The guest book should be attended until about ten minutes prior to the ceremony's starting, at which time the attendant should be seated by an usher or groomsman.

> ### Timeless Traditions
>
> Walking was once considered to be the best way of getting to the ceremony, since it afforded the bride a chance to see good omens. Rainbows, black cats, and chimney sweeps were all thought to be good luck.

Programs

EVEN at the simplest ceremony, guests should be provided with programs so that they'll be able to follow along with the service. (Although just as commonly, guests will be using the program to gauge when the ceremony will be over.) Programs may be made of anything from a simple sheet of paper printed on a laser printer to a booklet style of heavy cardstock embossed with the bride's and groom's initials. Programs should be given to each guest as they enter the ceremony site. Children too old to be flower girls/ring bearers but too young to be bridesmaids/groomsmen are particularly suited to the task of handing out programs. Program attendants should perform their task for the same amount of time that the guest-book attendant performs his, and likewise, should be seated about ten minutes prior to the ceremony's starting. Programs should include the entire service, along with the officiant's name (with explanations of particular customs or traditions if you'd like, particularly if all or part of the service is performed in a language other than the guests' native tongue), and should contain any readings so that guests may follow along. If your altar flowers or decorations are dedicated to someone's memory, it is correct to include that information at the end of the program.

Please take note that a wedding program is not a playbill; you may include the names of the wedding party but there is no need to indicate their relationship to you by printing the explanation "friend of the bride" (as opposed to "the bride's archenemy since grade school"?) next to their names. If you have honorary attendants, their names may be printed in the program, along with the reason for their absence. (See chapter 4 for more on honorary attendants.) There is no need to list the name of any vendor. Wedding directors and planners, musicians (although soloists should be listed in the service), floral designers, or anybody else who takes part in your ceremony in a purely professional capacity do not warrant a mention in the program. There is absolutely no need to list the names of relatives or anyone else who is not part of the wedding party—this includes parents. Keep in mind that the ceremony program should not be designed as a tool that alleviates you or anyone else of the responsibility of making proper introductions at the reception or in the receiving line.

This example of a program includes all the information necessary for a simple service:

Front Cover

The Marriage Celebration of
Julia Helen Phillips
to

Mr. John Christopher Haysworth
Saturday, the twenty-second of June
at seven o'clock
Saint Helena Episcopal Church
Beaufort, South Carolina

Left Inside Page

Order of Service
Celebrant: *Reverend Anthony Sgro*
Prelude: *Selections for Celtic Harp*
Bridesmaids' Processional: *"Canon in D
Minor," Pachelbel*
Bride's Processional: *"Trumpet Voluntary,"
Clark*

Opening Prayer
Scripture Reading : *Susan Spence:
Philippians 2:1-7*

Solo: *Liz Fordi
"Ave Maria," Schubert*

*The Greeting
Exchange of Vows
Exchange of Rings
Wedding Prayer
Pronouncement of Marriage
Benediction and Blessing*
Recessional: *"Ode to Joy," Beethoven*

Wedding Day Reflections

Prior to the ceremony, I was se-
questered with my bridesmaids at
the back of the church. I was hop-
ing for some quiet time with my
girlfriends, but it seemed like every
single relative of mine came in to
"say hi." I know they meant well,
but it was exhausting for me; I
didn't get to spend the time with
my bridesmaids that I wanted.
If I had to do it all over again,
I wouldn't have allowed anyone
else but my mom and mother-in-
law in the room.

—Liza

Right Inside Page

Wedding Party:

Maid of Honor:	Best Man:
Josie Osborne	*Paul McFaden*
Bridesmaids:	**Groomsmen:**
Diane Buckley	*Bruce Kirby*
Joanne Gibbs	*Steve Taylor*

Pre-Ceremony Photography

GENERALLY photographers are eager to accomplish as many of formal shots as possible prior to the ceremony. If the bride and groom choose not to see each other prior to the ceremony, the photographer will shoot the bride and her attendants separately from the groom and his. In order for pre-wedding photography to run smoothly, it is essential for everyone to arrive on time. The bride is the maid of honor's responsibility; the groom is the best man's. Attendants should use any means necessary, from setting watches fifteen minutes fast to making up false arrival times, to ensure that the bride and groom are on time.

There is no excuse whatsoever for the wedding party to be late; the same applies to parents or anyone else who is to appear in pre-wedding photography. The wedding party does not ask the limo driver to stop on the way so that they can buy beer, have a quick drink, or otherwise dilly-dally. The wedding party also does not show up with coolers loaded as if for a tailgate party. Once members of the wedding party arrive at the ceremony site, they should refrain from socializing unduly—the photographer requires complete cooperation.

Keep in mind that your photographer does not know any of your wedding party. It is therefore essential for the maid of honor, best man, and parents to introduce themselves to the photographer. This helps to prevent the photographer's staring blankly into the crowd yelling "Can I have the best man and the groom's parents up here?" Group shots by definition cannot be accomplished without the group in its entirety. For this reason, bridesmaids and groomsmen and anyone else scheduled to appear in pre-wedding photography should not go wandering off for any reason, including "to find a water fountain," "to go and fix my hair," or "to have a quick cigarette." Family, friends, and guests should kindly refrain from hanging around chatting to the wedding party while photography is underway.

Seating the Guests

GROOMSMEN and ushers who have been paying close attention the day before (see chapter 13 for more information on the rehearsal) should be able to perform their duties with aplomb. Groomsmen offer ladies their right arm and should seat guests as soon as they arrive, even if that's twenty minutes early. (It is very common for guests to arrive quite early, especially out-of-town guests, who, being unfamiliar with the city, give themselves *plenty* of time to get to the ceremony). Groomsmen seat friends and family of the groom on the right (facing the altar) and friends and family of the bride on the left. If there is a great discrepancy between the number of guests of the bride or groom, the tradition of asking "bride or groom" can certainly be done away with. Once the pre-ceremony photography is completed, relatives and whoever else is participating in the photography but not the wedding, may be seated. Once finished with photographs, the bride's and groom's parents should avoid the temptation to greet arriving guests; this only creates a cocktail-party atmosphere and causes a traffic jam into the ceremony site.

Who Escorts Whom?

THERE is no reason to assign a special escort to any guest, although of course a favorite grandson who is an usher may certainly be assigned to escort his grandmother. Brothers or relatives of the bride or groom who are either ushers or groomsmen are usually assigned to seat mothers. The best man should not usher any guest—the groom needs him.

Seating Family Members

FAMILY should be seated as soon as they are finished with photographs. Don't wait until everyone else is seated to seat grandparents or other close relatives; the idea is impractical and has no basis in etiquette. Family should be seated in the front rows, parents in the very front. There is no reason whatsoever why divorced parents cannot sit in the same pew. (There is not, by the way, any rule of etiquette that dictates specific seating arrangements at weddings.) Divorcees who simply cannot stand to sit near one another may quietly request that the usher seat them elsewhere.

Tardy Guests

ONCE the bride's mother has been seated, usually just a minute prior to the ceremony's start time, no other guest is seated by either an usher or groomsman. (Note: At Jewish weddings, the parents are not seated, rather they participate in the processional.) Tardy guests who've missed the ushers wait until the bride's mother is seated and very quickly and quietly sit in the back row, using the side rather than center aisle. Guests who arrive after the bride's processional at an open-air or tented wedding may *very* quietly be seated in the back. Guests who arrive at a ceremony underway in a building and find the doors closed should resign themselves to the fact that they've missed it and continue on to the reception. They do not open the (often large and creaky) doors and seat themselves, even in the back. In addition, tardy guests do not appear at the reception half an hour early and demand drinks from a bartender who is still setting up shop; they have no choice but to wait in their car at the reception site until they see the first guest arrive.

The Processional

IF the groomsmen are to walk out and assemble up front with the groom and officiant, they do so after the mother of the bride is seated. If they are to escort the bridesmaids or walk ahead of them, they assemble at this time also. Bridesmaids and groomsmen do not talk during the line-up unless they have something very important to say, then they whisper. (See chapter 8 for more information on the processional.)

The Receiving Line

THE receiving line is an old custom, one which affords you, the groom, the wedding party, and some of your family the opportunity to greet every guest. Although not practical for two hundred or more guests, a receiving line can work nicely for a smaller wedding. If you wish to have a receiving line, but are also planning to have post ceremony photographs taken at the ceremony site, you may do so in one of the following ways:

Should There Be a Receiving Line?

*My daughter is getting married next summer, and we're in the
preliminary planning stages. We're going to be having about
175 guests for a buffet reception. I would like to see them have a
receiving line, but she and her fiancé contend that a receiving
line is too "formal" and that they'd rather speak to everyone
during the reception. I think it's better to do that right after the
ceremony, rather than having guests practically lining up at the
reception anyhow to congratulate them. I'd also, as hostess, like
to greet all the guests, especially since I've never met most of my
future son-in-law's family or friends.*

What could possibly be "formal" about taking the time to greet all the guests
at a party? When your daughter invites friends to her house, does she simply prop
the front door open with a brick, allowing guests to wander freely in and out, un-
encumbered by introductions or farewells? I doubt it. You're right, a receiving
line forms all by itself; guests inevitably want to give their best to the newlyweds
(one does not properly congratulate the bride, only the groom). Family and
friends will also want to speak with you and the groom's mother, offering such
sentiments as: "What a lovely wedding, it just couldn't have been more perfect!"
or "How do you do? I'm Mark's second cousin from Sioux Falls." Friends of the
bride and groom will want to chat to the wedding party: "I just love your dress,

♦ If possible, you should arrange to have the reception cocktail
hour take place in a different setting than the main reception
(both, of course, would occur within the same site).

not 'bridesmaidy' at all!" "Nice tux man!" Unless there is a receiving line, guests are doomed to spend the better part of the reception figuring out how to get a word in edgewise. Even the determined, after hovering around the bride for twenty minutes (who is three deep in well-wishers), generally give up and head to the bar. They then feel obligated to renew their efforts before leaving, inevitably attempting to seek out the happy couple (now immersed in the conga line) to no avail. Guests then find themselves griping all the way home, "Three hours drive and we didn't even get a chance to say hi." The bride and groom, meanwhile, feel like they're running for public office, and the bride's parents have the sinking sensation that they've just spent several thousand dollars on a party for an inordinate number of complete strangers.

Herein lies the wisdom of the receiving line. You, as hostess, may greet all the guests at one time, as can the newlyweds, the mother of the groom, and the bridal party. The fathers may stand in the receiving line as they wish or mingle with guests. True, this process takes a little while, but after it is over, everyone feels as though they have said their piece and further introductions between the principals and guests are unnecessary. A receiving line also helps circumvent such cheery post-wedding commentary from the newlyweds as "We didn't even get a chance to eat," or, my personal favorite (and an impossibility had there been a receiving line), "We hardly knew anyone."

♦ When you arrive at the reception site from post ceremony photography you may form a receiving line to coincide with where guests enter the main reception location.

+ If your venue or reception style does not afford you two sites, you may have your receiving line at the ceremony site. Unless the weather is inclement, this is best accomplished by having those standing in the receiving line to do so outside the ceremony site.

If your guest list is large (125 to 200 or more) keep the receiving line to the bare minimum: The bride and groom, the honor attendants, and the bride and groom's mothers. If your guest list is manageable (125 and under) you may include your entire wedding party in the receiving line. The bride and groom's fathers may stand in the receiving line or proceed to the reception site to act as hosts if they wish. Those in the receiving line who know guests should introduce them to the others in the receiving line who don't: "John, this is Terry Andrews, she works with my friend Roland." Guests should congratulate the groom and wish the bride happiness (it is unseemly to congratulate the bride on landing a husband).

Although it is technically incorrect to organize a receiving line at a house of worship (since you cannot actually exclude anyone from a house of worship), lengthy post-wedding sessions with photographers have made these a necessity. If your guest list is large, do limit your receiving line to the bare minimum: The bride and groom, the honor attendants, and the bride and groom's mothers.

Post-Wedding Photography

IF you are not planning a receiving line, it is important that the entire wedding party and others who are to take part in photographs stay together after the ceremony. This may mean exiting the church or synagogue, then re-entering the room(s) in the back where everyone was getting ready prior to the ceremony. Wherever you assemble, it is

Dos & Don'ts

❧

Do try to have all guests sign the guest book at the ceremony site.

Do provide guests with programs.

Do arrive promptly for pre-wedding photography.

Do keep the entire wedding party together during photography.

Do have ushers/groomsmen seat guests as soon as they arrive.

Do keep the receiving line short if your guest count is large.

Don't use an expensive pen for guest book signing.

Don't list each member of the wedding party's relationship to you in the program.

Don't list parents in the program if they are not in the wedding party.

Don't use the best man as an usher.

essential that you stick together. It is imperative that no one gets stuck talking to guests on the front steps—this is a scenario from which it is impossible to escape. Post-wedding photography should not take more than thirty minutes to an hour, depending on the size of your wedding party and the number of formal shots you've requested. Again, as with pre-wedding photography, it is important that everyone pays attention and stays focused in order to expedite the process.

Etiquette for Friends and Guests

PUNCTUALITY is of utmost importance and guests who are "just always a little late for everything" should not expect a wedding to be delayed on their behalf. At the end of the ceremony, guests wait for the front pews to exit first and so on. They do not try to leave via the side aisle in order to be first at the bar at the reception. If there is a receiving line, guests do not attempt to circumvent it nor do they complain loudly while standing in line for the same. Friends keep their comments brief in the receiving line and always pretend to recognize strangers who obviously recognize them.

15

THE LIFE OF THE PARTY

ETIQUETTE AND THE RECEPTION

At last, the moment you've been waiting for, perhaps for a year or more—the chance to celebrate your marriage! The first social occasion you attend as husband and wife should reflect the love you feel for each other and the joy your guests feel for you both. A well-orchestrated wedding reception does not happen by chance. This chapter will clarify the proper order of events, from the receiving line to the bouquet toss. It will also help you create a realistic timeline (an essential) and answer questions such as: "When should we cut the cake?," "Is it all right to stay until the end of the reception?," "When should we start the first dance?," and "Do I have to toss my bouquet?"

Photography/Videography

These days, almost all the formal photographs are taken at the ceremony site. Those taken at the reception are seldom posed, but rather shot in a photojournalistic style. In general, neither photography nor videography should prove to be obtrusive during the reception. Photographers may carry with them as many business cards as they like. They may also ask the bride to spread the word that proofs will be available for viewing and ordering online within a month; they may not (the same applies to any vendor), however, set up trade-show-like displays at the reception. (See chapter 11 for more information on photography and videography.)

Creating the Timeline

IF you have retained a wedding planner, she should create a wedding timeline and provide it to vendors prior to your event. If you do not have a wedding planner, be sure to meet with your catering manager or reception-site contact person for help with creating your own. A timeline is essential if you want your reception to be well-organized and flowing smoothly. You must assign someone (such as your mother or your maid of honor) to alert you when it is necessary for you to participate in some activity (the cake cutting for instance). Give this person a copy of your timeline. When alerted, you must comply. Statements such as "Oh come on, not the cake now. We're having way too much fun. Come back in twenty minutes . . ." will only lead to chaos later on. The following is an example of a timeline designed to keep everyone informed and on-track.

Wedding Day Reflections

I *didn't think that much about my maid of honor giving a toast, so I hadn't planned on it or asked her to. But after the best man's toast, I sort of cajoled her into giving one, too. She hadn't prepared anything, which was pretty obvious. She said really nice things that were clearly from the heart, but if I had to do it over again, I would have asked her way ahead of time.*

—Diana

Timeline
(* Means announced by band/D.J., who also needs a copy of the timeline)

Julia Helen Phillips to John Christopher Haysworth
Saturday, June 22nd
7:00 P.M.
Saint Helena Episcopal Church (541-8290)
Reception
Pine Lakes Country Club (541-0006)
7:45 P.M. (approx.)
Wedding Planner's cell phone (541-2303)

4:00 P.M. Floral designer arrives at St. Helena to set up flowers, deliver bouquets/personal flowers.

5:00 P.M. Photographer's assistant arrives at St. Helena to shoot flowers/church.

5:30 P.M. Photographer arrives at the bride's house to shoot bride, family, bridesmaids.

6:00 P.M. Bride and maid of honor begin carriage ride from the bride's house to St. Helena, all others to follow in limo. Carriage driver to call wedding planner's cell prior to leaving house, as groom cannot see bride when she arrives at the church.

6:15 P.M. Photographer's assistant to arrive at St. Helena to shoot the groom/groomsmen and bride/bridesmaids separately.

6:40 P.M. Guests arrive.

7:00 P.M. Ceremony.

7:30 P.M. Ceremony ends.

7:45 P.M. Guests arrive at Pine Lakes Country Club, hors d'oeuvres passed, bars open.

7:45 P.M. Band starts.

8:00 P.M. Wedding planner to load gifts into the bride's father's car.

8:25 P.M. Wedding party to arrive at Pine Lakes Country Club.

8:30 P.M. Band announces bride and groom (Mr. and Mrs. John Haysworth).

8:35 P.M. Bride and groom's first dance ("Unforgettable").

8:40 P.M. Bride and bride's father dance ("Brown Eyed Girl").

8:45 P.M. Band breaks/buffet opens.

9:15 P.M. Band starts.

*9:30 P.M. Toast by the best man (Peter Fosselman).

*9:35 P.M. Band to announce bouquet presentation (bride to her grandmother, Mabel Sprinkle) immediately after best man's toast—no one else will be toasting.

*9:45 P.M. Cake cutting.

10:15 P.M. Band breaks.

*10:30 P.M. Bride and groom leave.

10:45 P.M. Photographer leaves, band starts.

11:45 P.M. Reception over, band ends, guests leave.

11:45 P.M. Floral designer and rental company arrive to tear down.

The Guest Book

IF it seems unlikely that everybody signed the guest book at the ceremony site (don't forget to have your family and wedding party sign), the book should be brought to the reception and set up, ideally, at the interior entrance to the ballroom or reception hall. In lieu of a traditional guest book, and sometimes in addition to the one signed at the ceremony site, couples are now conjuring up more creative ways to have their guests put good wishes into writing. Here are a few ways you can preserve your guests' sentiments:

- If you have menu cards printed for each person, have a separate card printed for each table that reads: *Please write a note for Julia and John on the back of your menu card.* Provide enough pens on each table to go around. If your place cards are large enough, you may use them for this purpose, too. After the wedding you can have the cards bound into little books.

- Have your engagement portrait matted with a wide mat. Set it up on an easel with a fine felt-tip pen so that guests can sign the mat when they enter your reception. Have the signed portrait framed after the reception.

- Choose a beautiful coffee table book and allow guests to sign and write notes on their favorite page.

- For a very small wedding, have guests sign a magnum (or larger) of champagne. Drink the champagne on your first anniversary.

- Set up a still camera at your reception so that guests can wish you well on film. This does not put guests on the spot in the same way that a videographer waving a microphone does.

Whichever type of guest book you choose, make sure that it is available as soon as guests arrive at the reception site, and encourage guests to sign as early as possible. It is not unheard of that, after three hours of partying, some guests' train of thought might not be particularly lucid, and their handwriting may not be entirely legible.

The Receiving Line

Now that post-wedding photography at the ceremony site prohibits the wedding party from arriving at the reception prior to guests, a receiving line at the reception is rare. If you are not planning to have post-ceremony photography, however, a receiving line at the reception is utterly correct, provided your guest list is not so large that it creates a long and slow moving bottleneck. By all means serve drinks and hors d'oeuvres butler-style to guests standing in line. Hors d'oeuvres should be served in a napkin and not require a plate. No one can shake hands with a glass in one hand and a plate in the other. (See chapter 14 for information about who should stand in the receiving line.)

Dealing with Gifts

ALTHOUGH it is a breech of etiquette for any guest to bring a gift to your wedding reception, more often than not, it happens. Reception sites are well-acquainted with this phenomenon and will usually provide a table on which guests may place their gifts. It is important that you plan ahead of time for someone to be responsible for loading the gifts into a pre-designated vehicle (the bigger the better). Gift loading should take place as soon as all guests have arrived at the site, placed their gifts on the table, and moved into the reception. Whoever is charged with loading should have a roll of scotch tape at the ready in order to tape envelopes to gifts. Envelopes notoriously part company with gifts making it impossible for the bride and groom to tell who gave what. It is also good thinking to provide a large box with a slit in the top for those who tempt fate by bringing gifts of cash or checks to the reception.

Cocktail Hour

IF the wedding party is involved in post-wedding photography at the ceremony site, which often delays their arrival at the reception site for up to an hour, it's a good idea to plan a cocktail hour, whether you choose to serve alcohol or not. During photography make sure that shots involving parents are taken first so that they are able to proceed to the reception site to mingle with guests prior to the wedding party's arrival.

Introductions

ALTHOUGH it is not necessary for the bride and groom to be introduced (since they have probably been presented as a couple at the end of the ceremony) it is a common practice and quite proper. Generally, the bandleader or DJ announces the couple as "Mr. and Mrs. John Haysworth" or if the bride is keeping her maiden name "Mr. John Haysworth and Ms. Julia Phillips." There is no need for the announcer to include such tidbits as "Appearing for the first time together as husband and wife . . ." You may choose to have your entire wedding party announced prior to you, which is correct, although not necessary. In any case, ask the DJ or bandleader to ask guests to hold their applause. Failure to do so creates a sort of Broadway play atmosphere, which can give rise to the feeling that the entire wedding party will join hands and bow to thundering applause while guests toss long-stemmed roses at their feet.

The First Dance

THERE is no set rule as to when the first dance should take place, however, many couples find it easiest to dance right after they've been announced. Traditionally, the bride danced with her father first, and the groom "cut in" about halfway through. Today the bride dances with the groom first to an entire song, then with her father to a different one. It's an exceptionally good idea for the bride and groom to take a few dance lessons before the wedding. While expectations should be kept low (the ambitious plan for the two of you to glide about the dance floor like Fred and Ginger is unlikely to eventuate), it's still prudent to brush up on a few steps, and perhaps learn something simple like a dip.

Some Perennial Favorites for the Bride and Groom Dance

"The Way You Look Tonight," Frank Sinatra

"At Last," Etta James

"Unforgettable," Nat King Cole

"What a Wonderful World," Louis Armstrong

"Moondance," Van Morrison

"You Send Me," Sam Cooke

"It Had to Be You," Frank Sinatra

OTHER IMPORTANT DANCES

If there is to be dancing at your reception, which is not a requirement, it is a must that the bride and groom dance with the groomsmen and bridesmaids and that groomsmen and bridesmaids dance with each other as well. The marital status of any member of the wedding party is irrelevant in relation to this rule. The bride should also dance with the groom's father, the groom with the bride's (and his own) mother. Obviously, married members of the wedding party should dance with their own spouses. There is no need for the band or DJ to orchestrate or announce any of these dances. They should occur as a matter of course.

Eating

IF the meal is plated, the bride and groom should sit down to the first course after the father-daughter dance (provided that cocktail hour is over). Dancing may occur between courses, or may cease until after dinner as you wish. At a buffet reception, dancing may occur throughout the reception or, more commonly, once everyone has had a chance to eat. The dance floor is ideally placed in the center of the room with tables arranged around it. Remember, if your reception space is large, but your guest count is comparatively small, resist the urge to space tables throughout the room. Guests like to be close to the dance floor and often feel alienated if they're seated far away from the action. However, if the band is loud, then of course it makes sense to provide seating as far away from the stage as is feasible for those who object to loud music (such as your elderly aunt with the hearing aid).

Wedding Day Reflections

I *wish I'd had someone at the reception who would have made us cut the cake on time. We were having so much fun we ended up not cutting it until 11:00 P.M. A lot of guests had left by then so we ended up with two whole tiers of leftover cake. The cake was really expensive and I regret that so much of it ended up going to waste.*

—Janice

Socializing

THE bride and groom and their parents should make every effort to say a few words to every guest if they have decided against a receiving line, which affords them the opportunity to do so prior to the reception. Even at a plated dinner, the bride and groom can table-hop between courses to accept guests' congratulations and best wishes and offer their own "thanks for coming." The bride and groom needn't go about together, in fact, it may be better if they don't, enabling them to rescue each another if either appears to be trapped in drawn-out dialogue. The best way to break in on a conversation is to say "Darling, I hate to tear you away, but the photographer needs us right now."

Toasts and Speeches

GENERALLY the bride's father welcomes guests at the beginning of the reception. If the officiant is present at the reception, she may offer the blessing. Otherwise anyone else may be asked to do the same. The best man offers a toast most logically between the end of the meal and the cutting of the cake. Champagne may be served for the toast or, just as correctly, guests may toast with whatever they happen to be drinking at the time. Before the best man toasts, it's important to request that the bride and groom come up front so that everyone can see their reaction and so forth. The bandleader or DJ should announce the toast, since it's difficult for amateurs to get everyone's attention. If a microphone is available, it's a good idea for the best man to use it, especially if there are many guests. After the best man, the maid of honor may toast; the bride and groom may also choose to say something. Toasting by an endless troupe of "inspired" guests becomes tedious very quickly so arrange that your band or DJ resume playing music at a specific time.

Cutting the Cake

As both an expensive and highly decorative item, the cake should be placed in a central location so that everyone is able to admire it. If the reception site is small or crowded and this is simply not possible, at least have the cake brought out to the dance floor so that everyone can see you cut it. Plan to cut the cake at a time that naturally coincides with dessert. Guests do not want to wait two hours after they've eaten for the cake. In the past, the bride and groom cut the cake shortly before their leaving. Today, when brides and groom stay until almost the end of the reception, this practice no longer makes sense. Traditionally, the bride and groom cut a slice of cake from the bottom layer—the groom feeds a piece to the bride, then vice versa. Squishing cake into each other's faces is not, and never has been, in good taste. Resist the temptation. The cake is then cut (by professionals, not the bride or groom) and served to each guest in the case of a plated meal. For a buffet or butlered hors d'oeuvres meal, the cake may be sliced and butlered to each guest, or it may be cut and placed on the buffet, in which case guests help themselves.

Wedding Day Reflections

I had instructed the band to announce the best man's toast at 9:30 P.M. A little before that I went to the powder room to fix my hair and put on lipstick. When I got back to the ballroom (at 9:29), I was shocked to find that not only had the best man toasted but also my maid of honor! The band didn't realize what a big difference announcing the toasts a few minutes early would make.

—Donna

The Groom's Cake

THE groom's cake is usually cut after the wedding cake without as much fanfare by the bride and groom or by the caterer. The cake is

How Much Wedding Cake?

&

I'm getting married in one month, and our guest count is pretty much finalized. We have retained a baker and soon need to let her know how many guests for the cake. Should we have one slice per guest? At $3.75 a slice and 170 guests, that's pretty steep. I've heard that a lot of people don't eat wedding cake, but I hate the thought of running out. Also, should we have a groom's cake? I've heard that this should be cut and boxed for guests to take home. Again at $2.75 a slice that's pretty expensive. To be honest, we've already spent most of our budget, and haven't really left ourselves quite enough money for this whole cake thing, which hasn't been in the forefront of our minds.

A wedding cake is absolutely essential to a reception and may be any flavor, color, or shape you wish. You should expect about 80% of your guests to eat wedding cake; however, in order to make your cake go a little further you should do two things. One, you should ask your caterer (or whoever will be cutting the cake) to serve small slices; two, you should not save the top layer. In the old days, as I discussed in chapter 9, wedding cakes (rich, dark fruitcakes) were saved to use as christening cakes. The kinds of cakes that modern brides serve do not lend themselves to being kept at room temperature for a year, nor do they

then served to guests in the same manner as the wedding cake. If the cake is to be boxed and given to the guests as a favor, it should be removed from the ballroom, sliced and boxed in the kitchen, then placed on a table from which guests can help themselves as they leave the reception.

freeze much longer than six months. Unless you want to pay $3.75 a slice to eat cake on your six-month anniversary or unless you plan to christen a child six months after your wedding, saving the top layer is a waste of money.

You may also consider another money-saving option. Have your baker make a very small wedding cake for you to cut (the bottom layer is the only one that needs to be real), then have her make a much less expensive sheet cake that can be cut in the kitchen and subsequently served to your guests. This is called "having your cake and eating it. too." A groom's cake is a charming idea, if your resources permit it. Typically it is made in a shape that represents an interest of the groom, a salmon for a fly fisherman, a football for a NFL fan, and so on. This cake may be served in addition to wedding cake or, as you say, be boxed as favors for the guests. This cake is not essential, and, since your resources are limited, may be omitted from your reception menu.

I realize that the wedding cake is not your top priority, but it is a very large part of your reception and highly photographed when you both cut it. A cake plays a large part in your decoration and is the focus of any buffet, often on a table decorated with yours and the bridesmaids' bouquets. It is important to remember that, although the bride and groom may not get to "eat a thing," most guests consider food and cake a top priority.

The Bouquet Toss

THE bouquet toss, an old tradition, is generally falling out of favor, although it is still quite common. The bouquet toss signals the bride

Presenting the Bouquet to Grandmother

I am thirty-seven years old (this is my first marriage) and am in the midst of planning my reception. All but a handful of my girl friends are married, including four out of my six attendants. My question is: Do I have to toss my bouquet? My single girlfriends groan at the idea; they think that they're just too old to participate in the tradition. I think it's pretty silly too. I've participated in many weddings during which we single women were rounded up and put in the spotlight, and I must admit, the older I was the more self-conscious I became about having my single status publicly announced. My grandmother is eighty-four years old and is flying all the way from Dublin, Ireland, for my wedding. What I'd like to do is give my bouquet to her. Should I have a separate "tossing" bouquet made for this or should I give her my actual bouquet? Also, at what time during the reception should I do this?

and groom's departure and should occur prior to when they plan to leave. The bandleader or DJ may announce the toss and all single ladies of any age may choose to participate. The bride stands with her back to the ladies assembled and tosses the bouquet over her head, making no overt attempt to target any one lady in particular (which is not good sportsmanship). Ladies should make a restrained effort to catch the bouquet, and they should keep in mind that it is not a home-

The tossing of the bouquet is an old tradition but, for the reasons you mentioned, one that is falling out of favor, particularly with more mature brides. The idea that all single women are dying to be married ASAP is one whose time has come and gone. Giving your bouquet to your grandmother, who will obviously make quite an effort to attend your wedding, is a charming gesture. If you are planning to have your bouquet preserved, by all means have your floral designer make you a tossing bouquet. If, however, you are not going to keep your bouquet, present her with the real thing. Since your grandmother may not wish to stay at the reception until you leave, when the bouquet is usually tossed, you should endeavor to schedule the presentation earlier in the reception, ideally after the best man gives his toast. You should make a little speech, heartfelt but not lengthy (the same goes for all speeches or toasts made at your reception), after which you should simply give the bouquet to your grandmother. You may wish to have all or part of your bouquet preserved for her. Placing the bouquet in water for the remainder of your reception will ensure that the blooms remain fresh. Be certain to let your photographer/videographer know about your plans. The look on your grandmother's face when you give her the most important flowers of your life will be one you'll want to have captured on film forever.

run ball and the vigorous efforts that are necessary to secure such a trophy are not considered dignified at a wedding.

The Garter Toss

THIS custom is seen less and less these days and has never been a particularly charming one. If you are going to toss the garter, its removal should be accomplished with as much good taste as one can possibly muster while stripping a lady of an undergarment in public. The playing of striptease music while this is taking place does not elevate the activity to a higher plane. As with the bouquet toss, single gentlemen of all ages congregate to catch the garter, and the groom throws it with his back to them. The custom of the garter recipient sliding the same onto the thigh of the bouquet recipient is tasteless and usually embarrassing for both involved.

Handling Leftovers

MOST reception sites must comply with laws that usually prohibit their allowing anyone to leave the premises with leftover food. (Most, however, should prepare a basket of food and cake for you and the groom to take.) Check ahead of time, and, if they will allow leftovers to be taken, make sure that you assign someone to be responsible for them and for the top layer of your cake, if you're keeping it. You may also arrange for leftover food to be taken to a shelter or other nonprofit agency; check with your catering manager to see if that's feasible. Flowers (but not their containers) may be distributed among guests at the end of the reception, unless the containers are disposable (most plain glass containers are considered disposable, but check first). Be sure to let the catering staff know that guests may remove the flowers but not the containers. (Flowers in nondisposable containers are usually arranged in floral foam that is then taped onto plastic saucers, which are easily removed from the containers. Most large buffet centerpieces are arranged in this fashion.) It is a very nice gesture to reserve some centerpieces to be given to the servers who have worked your wedding reception. This cannot, however, be construed as a tip. (See chapter 2 for more information on tipping.) If you wish for your centerpieces to be taken to hospitals, nursing homes, or shut-ins, arrange for pickup and delivery with your floral designer ahead of time.

Leaving

ALTHOUGH couples nowadays wait until almost the end (or even the very end) of their reception to leave, this is technically not correct etiquette. The proper time to leave is about an hour before the end of the reception, when the party is in full swing. The band or DJ should announce your leaving so that guests may assemble outside with whatever they've been given to toss. If you and the groom are changing into "going away" outfits (usually reserved for couples who are leaving for their honeymoon immediately after the reception), do so prior to the band's announcement.

Check with your reception site to see what they will allow guests to toss—some venues are quite strict. The most common tossing items are rose petals and birdseed. Bubble blowing is also popular, particularly if there are many children present. A nice alternative, particularly if you are leaving in the dark, is to provide your guests with sparklers (and the matches with which to light them); this makes for a very pretty exit. Although the releasing of butterflies has gained popularity, it's a good idea to call your local extension agent and find out if the species you are to release will have any adverse affect on indigenous species of butterflies or other insects.

You should instruct your band or DJ to play very upbeat music after your departure. This will signal to your guests that the party will continue and that they should not feel obligated to leave.

When to Leave the Reception

❧

I'm getting married in a few weeks, and a friend has recommended that I make up a schedule or timeline for the reception. The reception—which will be heavy, buffet-style hors d'oeuvres and a full bar and dancing—begins at 5:00 P.M. and lasts until 9:00 P.M. We'll be having some pictures taken beforehand, so we expect to arrive at about 5:45 P.M. What time should we cut the cake? Throw the bouquet? (Also my fiancé wants to do the whole garter thing, which I'm not really comfortable with, but he says it's tradition etc., etc.) When should the best man make his toast? My father would like to make a toast, too; when would be a good time? We don't have to fly out for our honeymoon until the following morning, so is it OK that we stay at the reception until the end? Many of our friends are flying in for the wedding, so we'd really like to spend as much time with them as possible.

Your friend has made a very sound recommendation. It is unwise to just let the evening take its course since that may mean the best man's being in the bathroom at toast time and the cake's being cut at 8:59 P.M. Making out a simple timeline and handing copies to the bandleader/DJ, caterer, photographer, and your maid of honor and best man will prevent chaos and keep your reception fun. Given that the reception begins at 5:00 P.M., the best man should make his toast at about 6:45 P.M. By then, most people will be finished with their hors d'oeuvres and will *also have a glass of champagne, or whatever libation you've chosen, for the toast. However, you should work closely with your caterer concerning this timeline, particularly if champagne is to be served butler style. Your father may make a toast after the best man's, preferably immediately, when it will be easy to maintain your guests' attention and glasses are still, optimistically, half full. Your father may also choose to welcome guests at the beginning of the reception. This is not a requirement, but certainly a nice touch. At about 7:00 P.M. you should cut the cake (again, let your caterer advise you, since her staff will be the ones actually serving the cake, a task which can be quite time-consuming, depending on the number of guests). When everyone has had their cake and, if your baker is good, eaten it, too, the garter toss may commence. The garter toss is an old tradition, slightly embarrassing at best, tasteless at worst; it may be omitted from your reception festivities with impunity. However, if you choose to take part in this ritual, do so immediately prior to your tossing the bouquet. The bouquet toss is a signal of your impending departure and should be accomplished before many guests begin to leave, at about 7:45 P.M. By "impending" I do not mean an hour and forty-five minutes later, when the band is packing up and the caterers are removing the tablecloths. It has become more and more common for the bride and groom to stay at the reception until the very end, which tends to give the impression that no post-wedding activity can afford them keener pleasure than partying with friends. Unless you are quite happy to permit your guests this unfortunate perception of you and the groom, leave by 8:00 P.M. If, after two hours worth of reception, out-of-town friends have not had their fill of you and vice versa, by all means arrange to meet them later. The next morning, at the airport, for breakfast.*

After Parties

IF the wedding takes place during the day, it's a common practice for the bride's parents to invite some close friends and family to dinner afterwards. This is not a requirement, but it's a nice gesture, especially if out-of-town guests are included. If the wedding takes place in the evening, it is also common for the bride's parents to host a brunch or luncheon the following day. Again, this is certainly not a must, merely a charming way to wrap up a wonderful weekend.

Etiquette for Friends and Guests

GUESTS should not bring wedding gifts of any kind to the reception. If they do so, they should be prepared to accept the consequences: gifts separated from envelopes, lost gifts, or envelopes inadvertently thrown away. If there is a receiving line at the reception, guests queue without complaint and do not, under any circumstances, attempt to circumvent the line. When greeted by the bride or groom at the reception, guests do not monopolize their time. Instead, they keep congratulations and best wishes brief.

Guests do not ask for leftovers to be wrapped up for them (if leftovers are allowed to be taken off the premises, they're probably already spoken for), nor do they attempt to coerce bartenders into giving them opened bottles of liquor or wine, generally these belong to the reception site or caterer. If the bride and groom have provided their own drinks, no doubt they've arranged for someone to take the surplus. Guests do not hang around the reception site after the party is over attempting to have the bartender make them "one for the road." If guests feel they have not socialized sufficiently, by all means they should arrange to go out with other guests.

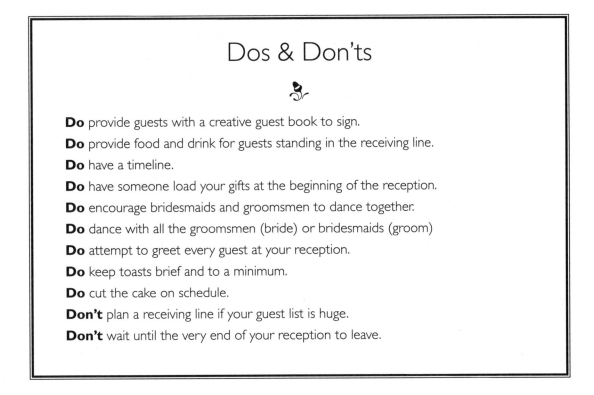

Dos & Don'ts

Do provide guests with a creative guest book to sign.

Do provide food and drink for guests standing in the receiving line.

Do have a timeline.

Do have someone load your gifts at the beginning of the reception.

Do encourage bridesmaids and groomsmen to dance together.

Do dance with all the groomsmen (bride) or bridesmaids (groom)

Do attempt to greet every guest at your reception.

Do keep toasts brief and to a minimum.

Do cut the cake on schedule.

Don't plan a receiving line if your guest list is huge.

Don't wait until the very end of your reception to leave.

Guests may take centerpieces if they've been given permission (usually by the bride, her mother, or the catering manager); however, they do not remove nondisposable containers along with the flowers. Guests who have had too much to drink ask the catering manager to call them a cab home.

Etiquette for After the Wedding

If there is an event held in your honor the day after the wedding, it is imperative that you and the groom arrive on time. This does not mean at noon for a brunch that was planned from 9:00 to 12:00. Even if you're horribly tired/hungover/cranky, you must listen to friends' and family's congratulations and best wishes all over again with good humor and good gratitude, and be prepared to rehash the entire reception.

Be sure to put your dress in good hands. It will need to be dropped off for cleaning and preserving as soon as possible. Don't wait until after your honeymoon to accomplish this—stains will be much more difficult to remove by then. Also make sure the groom's tuxedo is delivered to the dry cleaners or taken back to the rental company on time. Aside from that, enjoy the honeymoon—and *write your thank-you notes!*

INDEX

A

Admission cards, 101

Announcements
  couple generated,
    16–18
  formal, 119
  general, 13
  special circumstances
    deceased parent,
      13–15
    divorced bride, 16
    divorced parent,
      16–18
    widowed bride, 15

At-home cards, 119, 122

Attendants. *See also* specific
    roles
  children as, 66–67
  choosing, 57–60
  firing, 73–74
  gifts for, 74–75
  honor, 61–62
  matching, 60
  out clause, 60
  outfits, 62–66
  personal appearance, 62
  responsibilities, 72–73
  seating at reception,
    187–190
  symbolism, 69

Attire
  attendants, 62–66
  black-tie dilemma,
    51–54
  formal weddings, 48–50
  informal weddings, 50
  masters of ceremonies,
    192
  musicians, 192
  second marriages, 51
  semiformal weddings,
    50–51
  very formal weddings,
    47–48

B

Bachelor/ bachelorette
    parties
  coed, 226–227
  costs, 227
  dos & don'ts, 234
  gifts, 230
  guest for, 227, 230
  guests etiquette,
    234–235
  planning, 226, 228–229
  single sex, 226
  tasteful, 232–233
  themes, 231
  tradition of, 225
  transportation, 230–231

Bands, 191

Bars
  B.Y.O.B., 185
  cocktail hours, 275
  controversy, 184
  full, 181–183
  glassware, 185–186
  no host, 188–189
  theme, 185

Best man
  attire, 63, 66
  flowers for, 202
  responsibilities, 70–72

Bribery, 31, 34

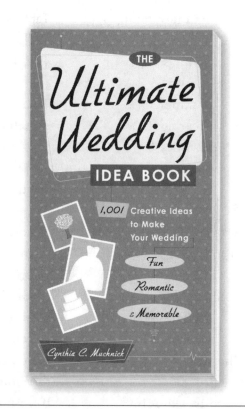